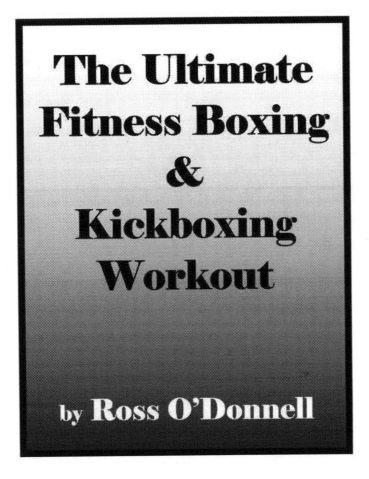

The Ultimate
Fitness Boxing
&
Kickboxing
Workout

by Ross O'Donnell

Demonstration Photographs of Joanne O'Donnell Certified Personal Trainer & Ross O'Donnell
Photographs taken at Bryon Mackie's Bigtyme Fitness & Boxing, Orangeville

Order this book online at www.trafford.com
or email orders@trafford.com

Most Trafford titles are also available at major online book retailers.

Print information available on the last page.

ISBN: 978-1-4120-6451-4 (sc)
ISBN: 978-1-4122-3818-2 (e)

Trafford rev. 02/12/2019

www.trafford.com

North America & international
toll-free: 1 888 232 4444 (USA & Canada)
fax: 812 355 4082

Dedicated
To
My parents
Ross Sr. and Lorraine O'Donnell

Special thanks to the following people who, each in their own way provided me
with the motivation and encouragement to complete this book:
Brittany O'Donnell
Len O'Donnell
Janice Shepherd
Catherine & Kaitlyn Schneider
Bruce & Doreen Barber

TABLE
OF
CONTENTS

CHAPTER ONE
Introduction
About the Book 1
Introduction to New Instructors 2
Fitness Benefits to Participants 2
Goal Setting and Recognition........................3
History of Fitness Boxing & Kickboxing 4

CHAPTER TWO
Getting Started
The "Do it Yourself" Fitness Test 5
Calculate Your Target Heart Rate....................6
Back to the Basics 6
SMART Fitness Goals 8
Putting Your Best Foot Forward....................9
Calculating Your Body Mass Index 9
Keeping a Fitness Journal 10

CHAPTER THREE
Warm-Up & Stretching
Warm-Up 11
Stretching 101 12
Stretch Your Quality of Life............................12

CHAPTER FOUR
Resistance Training
Muscling Up....................................15
Don't Resist Resistance Training....................16
Resistance Training....................................16
Super-Sets for Fitness....................................17
Muscle Building Guidelines............................18
Fitness Circuit Training Routine 18
Smart Fitness Tips for Dumbbells...................19
Get on the Ball and Get Fit 20
Pilates + Stability Ball = Results 21
Medicine Ball Training 22

CHAPTER FIVE
Cardio Training
Heart Health 23
Training the Right Energy 23
Running for Fitness....................................24
Walking Your Way to Fitness........................25

CHAPTER SIX
Abdominals
Flat Abs on Time....................................27
Abs 28
More Ab Work....................................28

CHAPTER SEVEN
Boxing & Kickboxing
Fitting Martial Arts into Fitness Training..........29
The Punch and Kick Workout 30

CHAPTER EIGHT
Fitness for Any Age
Fitness Over 40 31
Older Adult Fitness Tips 31
Physical Activity for Children and Youth 32
Youth Sports Training = Training for Life 33

CHAPTER NINE
Nutrition & Hydration
Helpful Hydration Hints 35
Proper Nutrition + Exercise = Results.............36
Your Calorie Counting Calculation...................37

CHAPTER TEN
Helpful Fitness Tips
Sleeping Your Way to Health and Fitness 39
Injuries - Prevention and Treatment.................40
FAQ - Fitness Clubs vs Home Gyms 41
Choosing a Personal Trainer 41
Winter Cold Weather Exercise Tips 42
Summer Hot Weather Exercise Tips................43
Fitness Motivation Tips.................................43
"Two of a Kind" Partner Training.....................44
Fit-Break for the Home Based Business..........45
Taking Vacation Time for Yourself...................46

CHAPTER ELEVEN
Equipment & Hand Wrapping
Guidelines for Equipment Selection.................47
Hand Wrapping..49

CHAPTER TWELVE
Punching & Kicking Techniques
Fighting Stance...................................51
The Jab...52
The Cross...52
The Hook 53
The Uppercut 54
The Lead Leg Front Snap Kick 55
The Roundhouse Kick (Lead Leg).....................56
The Rear Leg Front Snap Kick 57
The Knee Strike..58

CHAPTER THIRTEEN
Pad Holding & Heavy Bags
  Kicks: Pad Holding & Foot Placement
    For Round/Roundhouse Kick 59
    For Snap Kick and Knee Strike 59
  Kicks: Fighter & Pad Holder Positions
    Fighting Stance & Pad Holder Stance 60
    Lead Leg Front Snap 60
    Rear Leg Front Kick 61
    Lead Leg Round Kick 61
    Rear Leg Roundhouse Kick 62
    Rear Leg Knee Strike 62
  Evasive Techniques: Fighter & Pad Holder
    Step Out Evasive Technique 63
    Slip a Left Jab 63
    Slip a Right Cross 64
    Duck a Hook 64
  Punches: Pad Holding & Foot Placement
    Jab, Cross, Hook & Uppercut 65
  Punches: Boxer & Pad Holder Positions
    Jab & Cross 66
    Hook & Uppercut 67
  Heavy Bag Punches
    Jab, Cross, Hook & Uppercut 68

CHAPTER FOURTEEN
Boxing Combinations
  Eight Sample Boxing Combinations 69

CHAPTER FIFTEEN
Kickboxing Combinations
  Eight Sample Kickboxing Combinations 77

CHAPTER SIXTEEN
Agility Exercises
  Agility Ladder Exercises
    In-In-Out-Out 85
    Hop Scotch 86
    Side Step Shuffle 86
  Agility Weave Poles 87
  Mini-Hurdles 87

CHAPTER SEVENTEEN
Resistance Training Exercises
  Lower Body Exercises
    Seated Leg Extension Front Kick 89
    Squat & Lunge 90
    Side Kick & Roundhouse Kick 91
    Squeeze & Punch 92
    Side-Step 93
    Rear Kick 94
  Upper Body Exercises
    Bench Press 94
    Flyes & Seated Lat Row 95
    Seated Two Arm Row & Bicep Curl 96
    Tricep Extensions 97
    Seated Overhead Press & Side Laterals 98
    Front Delt Raise & Reverse Flyes 99
  Pilates
    Shoulder Exercise 100
    Shoulder & Bicep Exercise 101

Resistance Training Exercises (Continued)
  Optional Warm-Ups
    Resistance Tubing - Jab/Cross 102
    Resistance Tubing - Uppercut 103
  Abdominal Workouts
    Toe Tappers 103
    Side-to-Side 104
    Jack Knifes & Roll-Ups 105
    V-Sit Bicycles 106
    Heal to Toe Punches 107
    Up & Out 108
    One Legged Plank 109
    One Armed Plank 109
    Side Oblique Plank 110
    One Legged Plank with Knee Strike 110
    Oblique Plank with Elbow Touch 110

CHAPTER EIGHTEEN
Stretching Exercises
  Glutes, Groin, Hamstrings & Adductors 111
  Hamstrings, Calves, Shin-Anterior Tibialis,
    Groin, Quads, , & Glutes 112
  Back, Shoulders & Rear Deltoids 112
  Obliques, Top Deltoids & Trapezius 113
  Full Upper Body Stretch 114
  Obliques & Rear Deltoids 116

CHAPTER NINETEEN
Sample Workout
  Warm-Up, Stretching & Resistance 117
  Optional Cardio Combinations 118
  Pad Drills - Punching & Kicking 119
  Beginner Combinations 120
  Bag Training Combinations 121
  Abs, Back & Upper Body Floor Exercises 122
  Stretching 122

CHAPTER TWENTY
Beginner Workouts & Journals
  Warm-Up & Combinations 123
  Resistance Training Exercises 124
  Short-Term & Long-Term Goals 125
  Daily Journal 126
  Workout Chart 127

CHAPTER TWENTY-ONE
Contender Workouts & Journals
  Warm-Up & Combinations 129
  Resistance Training Exercises 130
  Short-Term & Long-Term Goals 131
  Daily Journal 132
  Workout Chart 133

CHAPTER TWENTY-TWO
Champ Workouts & Journals
  Warm-Up & Combinations 135
  Resistance Training Exercises 136
  Alternate Split Routine Workouts 137
  Short-Term & Long-Term Goals 138
  Daily Journal 130
  Workout Chart 140

CHAPTER ONE

Introduction

....

About the Book

Welcome to the 21st century where we have become a society of "multi-taskers" and can incorporate that mind set into our fitness training. Over the last few years boxing and kickboxing have become popular forms of fitness training in North America for those looking to progress beyond the Tae-Bo, aerobic-kickboxing and boxercise type formats.

This book details how to get a calorie burning cardiovascular and resistance workout combined with learning valuable self-defense skills. The routines are also dynamite ways to build self-confidence, agility, coordination, stamina and relieve stress.

Complete with a wide variety of topical information on both general and specific components of fitness, it is professionally detailed with over 300 photographs depicting every punch and kick technique combination. From the warm-up, strength exercises, ab routines and cool down stretches it is designed to ensure safety and efficiency in planning your fitness regiment.

The exercises are fully explained, and sample workouts are provided allowing you to determine the intensity of your workout based on your fitness and skill level. Tailored to your goals, it makes an ideal, fresh, innovative and personalized workout.

The training can be structured into two or three minute rounds with 30 to 60 second rests to replicate actual boxing and kickboxing rounds, enhancing mental focus by concentrating on the various, challenging and stress relieving kick and punch combinations. It can also be implemented as the cardio portion or warm-up to your regular routine or as an additional alternate session format tailored to your goals and needs.

All the equipment required, like boxing gloves, heavy bags and focus pads are portable and the initial expenditure is fairly modest compared to elaborate home gyms. The additional strength and resistance exercises incorporating the stability ball, medicine ball, resistance tubing and free body exercises keep the program unique, easy to modify and can be taken with you when traveling or at work.

So grab your wraps and gloves and get ready to punch, kick, bob and weave your way to fitness.

Introduction to New Instructors

A fitness boxing or kickboxing program consists of a two to three hour educational workout, intended to introduce the participant to the fitness benefits derived from fitness boxing and kickboxing. Boxing gloves and wraps are recommended and foot and shin guards optional. No one should ever strike heavy bags without proper hand protection.

The class starts with a warm up cardio exercise of either air attack moves or a skipping workout. The Instructor then demonstrates the proper techniques to be utilized during the session ahead. The participants/instructor will select partners with consideration for the opponent's size (the partners will be of similar height, weight, fitness and skill level). This segment of the workout will be used to practice good boxing and kickboxing techniques.

The session then moves into strike, kick and punch combinations structured in two or three minute rounds to simulate a competitive match. Round timers signify the start and end of each round with a 30 to 60 second rest and water break. During each round, one partner will be the striker and one the defender/pad holder. Each combination will be predetermined so that both partners are aware of and prepared for the routine.

A more vigorous workout is utilized for advanced classes and participants are able to work in partners on more complex combinations or on free-standing heavy bags. (Optional sparring classes can be made available for advanced participants.)

All classes conclude with strength, abdominal and back exercises followed by stretching.

Fitness Benefits to Participants

- Fat Loss
- Stress Relief
- Flexibility
- Easy to Learn
- Individual Instructions
- Toning
- Safety
- Variety
- Self-Confidence

Back in the 1950's there were those exercise machines with belts that were supposed to shake the fat away. Thankfully we moved forward from there. In the 80's and 90's fitness enthusiasts flocked to clubs for aerobic step training. Times and trends are changing again. Welcome to the 21st century where we have had the good fortune of being introduced to new and fabulously effective training methods such as Pilates and the Stability Ball.

Through vast resources via the internet, you have the opportunity to educate yourself on a variety of new and innovative techniques and fitness programs. We have become a society of "multi-taskers" so why not incorporate that mind set into our fitness training. Over the last couple of years boxing and kickboxing have become some of the most popular forms of fitness training in North America. The reason for this is, you get the best cardiovascular and resistance workout ever and learn valuable self-defense skills all at the same time. Although sparring is an option for advanced students, 98% of participants join strictly for the fitness. Like boxing classes, that have become immensely popular, fitness boxing and kickboxing offer the opportunity to train like a real boxer or kickboxer, gaining all the benefits without having to get in the ring.

Studies conducted have revealed that a 45-60 minute boxing or kickboxing class can burn off 600-800 calories.

In addition to the weight loss, you are building lean muscle which raises your metabolism burning calories at rest and toning the whole body. The kicking exercises concentrate on the thighs, hips and buttocks unlike any other workout. By utilizing partner training you get the increased motivation and commitment that makes it ideal for couples wanting to workout together or regular training partners of any age or fitness level. Unlike the traditional aerobics class where everyone is staying at the same pace, your intensity is determined by you and your partner.

The use of focus pads and heavy bags provides a tremendous form of resistance training that again builds lean muscle and has the additional perk of increasing bone density.

The partner training is structured into two or three minute rounds to replicate actual boxing or kickboxing rounds in a competition and is a dynamite way to build skill and stamina. The mental aspect of the training builds self confidence knowing that you can defend yourself as well as a stress reliever being able to blow off some steam after a long day.

Once you've learned the basics, the combinations are endless providing for constant variety in your routine. The stretching exercises that are an integral part of boxing and kickboxing training enhance flexibility and range of motion that are so crucial in our everyday lives. Boxing and kickboxing are also great ways to improve agility, endurance and coordination to carry over to other sports.

So kick start your fitness program today with a routine that packs a punch!

Goal Setting and Recognition

As in most training and fitness programs, participants are divided into three categories: Beginners, Contenders (intermediate) and Champs (advanced). Fitness boxing and kickboxing are designed adhering to proper techniques and fitness related benefits, which usually can be realized within six to twelve months. Unlike martial arts that take years of diligent training to attain proficiency and ascend through the rank belt structure, fitness kickboxing is designed adhering to self-defense techniques and, again, the associated fitness related benefits are often realized within six to twelve months.

Like many other fitness programs that offer pins, certificates of accomplishments and other forms of recognition, fitness boxing and kickboxing can offer an incentive or recognition program.

The recognitions are established at the discretion of the club/instructor on the basis of the participant demonstrating basic techniques in accordance with their level of training, fitness improvement and adherence to all aspects of the program. The levels provide for short-term and long-term establishment in goal-setting over a twelve month period and longer.

It is generally accepted that fitness training yields its most noticeable benefits in the first eight to twelve weeks. Therefore the Beginner program should be structured over a two to three month period. Once you can demonstrate basic competence in the prescribed techniques, (2-3 move combinations) and are progressing towards your own fitness goals you can move on to the Contender workouts.

Introduction

The Contender level usually lasts from twelve to twenty weeks, and implements more physically challenging training and combinations (3-4 move combinations).

Finally, the Champ level incorporates much more complex and physically demanding cardio vascular and muscle movement patterns as well as *optional sparring**.

NOTE: * ***Boxing Sparring***:

Only under the supervision of a trained certified boxing coach in accordance with Boxing Ontario & C.A.B.A. rules at recognize registered Boxing Clubs.

* ***Kickboxing Sparring***:

Only under the supervision of a trained sport kickboxing instructor or martial arts instructor and subject to club rules.

History of Fitness Boxing & Kickboxing

In the 1990's, "Boxercise" aerobic classes became very popular but left the participants wanting to advance their workouts without actually getting in the ring to compete. By the late 1990's real boxing and boxing workouts had begun to reach the mainstream. However, there was a lack of quality highly trained professionals and clubs to conduct these intense workouts.

Kickboxing has its roots in martial arts and began as a sport in North America in the early 1970's as a full contact combat sport alternative to karate competition. The attraction is the full contact aspect of the sport of kickboxing which combines boxing punches and martial arts kicks. To properly learn and improve in kickboxing you must learn to box and to kick. Martial artists becoming involved in kickboxing soon adopted the boxing stance as opposed to the traditional bladed (sideways stance) which is awkward and ineffective in the

sport. Rules and protective equipment were implemented due to increased risk of injury, but the sport is still not sanctioned in many parts of North America including Ontario.

People began trying fitness boxing and kickboxing as alternatives to the "traditional gym" and have found the most fun, motivating and challenging workouts that they have ever experienced.

Relieve your frustrations from the workday and vent your aggressions as you punch, kick, bob and weave your way into the best shape of your life. Experience the thrill of hitting a heavy bag, punching a focus pad and kicking a shield while learning self defense. Jump rope, work the speed-bag, shadow box, complete the agility kickbox-circuit or work on the core stability ball strength training exercises designed to rip killer abs, tone your muscles, build your endurance and shape your physique.

CHAPTER TWO

Getting Started

The "Do it Yourself" Fitness Test - Before You Start

Many people want to start a fitness program at home and keep track of their progress but aren't sure how to determine their current fitness levels with regards to strengths and weaknesses. To conduct your own test requires no special equipment and allows you to record your personal results. The results will give you a bench mark as to where you started, strengths and weaknesses, motivate, assist in the goal setting and give you a way to evaluate and direct your exercise routine. The following is a very simplified home fitness test you can perform yourself. You want to include cardiovascular endurance, core, upper and lower body strength and flexibility. _Remember_ since you are just starting a fitness program _don't_ _overdo_ _it_. Safety is the most important factor.

1. Cardiovascular Endurance:

You can walk or run a pre-measured one-mile distance and time yourself. To check on improvements after you have started a program repeat the same testing procedure later and compare the time it took to walk or run the mile.

2. Upper Body:

Push-ups are a good indicator of upper body strength. Perform either male or female (from the knees) style pushups, going, all the way down until your nose almost touches the floor and all the way up until your arms are fully extended. Do as many as you can and log the score.

3. Core, Abdominals & Back:

Partial sit-ups are to be performed by lying on your back on the floor; legs are at 90 degree angles with the soles of your feet flat on the ground. Place your palms on your thighs and, by contracting your abs, raise your torso upward until you bring your fingers to the top of your knees. Do as many as you can with proper form and log the score.

4. Lower Body:

Squats can be an easy indicator. Sit at the edge of a chair on which your knees are at right angles to the floor. Stand up and sit back down just barely touching the chair and immediately stand back up. Repeat until you cannot properly perform any more repetitions then log the score.

5. Flexibility:

Stand with your feet together and legs perfectly straight, bend at the waist and keep your palms parallel to the floor. Log how close you come to placing your palms flat on the floor.

Perform all the components of the test again in eight weeks to monitor your progress.

Calculating Your Target Heart Rate Training Zone
Target Heart Rate = 220 – Age x Range

Range = (60% to 90% of Max. Heart Rate)
bpm = Beats per minute

Beginners and less fit individuals should strive for 60-70% of maximum heart rate and more fit experienced exercisers should strive for 70-90%.

Example : 20 year old beginner
220 - (Age) 20 X 0.60
= 120 bpm (60%)
0.70 = 140 bpm (70%)

Divide the beats per minute by six to give you your beats per 10-second count.

You can check periodically during your workout by stopping and placing your finger on the carotid artery in your neck and counting the beats for 10 seconds to ensure you are staying in your target heart range.

Back to the Basics - The Components of Fitness

Many times fitness enthusiasts get caught up in advanced or sport specific training programs and forget about the basics. Beginners need to learn proper form and technique to build on. Advanced participants can sometimes take a step back to the basics to correct newly acquired bad habits.

There are four primary areas of concern and five secondary factors affecting your total fitness level. Keep in mind that each must be considered to attain overall fitness.

Primary Components of Fitness
1. Body Composition :

This refers to the proportion of lean mass compared to fat. This is often equated to Body Mass Index (BMI). A high BMI reading, generally over 27, is associated with many health related risks including heart disease, high cholesterol, diabetes etc. See "Muscle Building Guidelines" on page 18.

2. Resistance Training :

This can involve traditional weight training with machines or free weights. It can also be accomplished by using free body exercises or stability ball training.

Target your training sessions to meet your goals, usually 2-3 times a week. To tone, keep the resistance light and the reps high, 12-15. To build, keep the number of reps lower, 8-10 and the resistance heavy. Resistance training improves posture, prevents and reduces the likelihood of osteoporosis and reduces loss of muscle due to aging. See Chapters Four and Seventeen.

3. Cardiovascular Training :

Try to keep physically active 30 minutes a day with walking, biking or whatever you enjoy that will give your heart a workout. For training purposes train 3-5 times a week in your target heart rate zone. See "Calculating your Target Heart Rate Training Zone" above. Cardiovascular fitness reduces the risk of heart disease, normalizes the blood pressure and lowers the resting heart rate.

4. Flexibility Training :

This should be done before and after each training session. Before working out, utilize dynamic stretching mimicking the routine you are about to perform and keep the range of motion to 75%. After your exercises, with warm muscles perform full body stretching ensuring that you exhale while lengthening the muscles and hold each stretch for at least 10-30 seconds. Stretching also helps restore the natural length to the tendons and ligaments as well as reduces incidence of injury during training or everyday tasks. See Chapter Eighteen.

Secondary Components of Fitness

These involve skills and abilities such as balance, coordination, agility, reaction time, speed and mental capacity (to train). Whether you are an elite athlete or just starting a fitness program, everyone can gain sports performance enhancement or better everyday functionality by improving these components. Whatever your motivation is to stay fit or get in shape, start off with a well-balanced program, sticking to the basics and building slowly to ensure a safe and efficient routine.

Some people are training for muscle mass, some for weight loss, increased cardiovascular efficiency, strength or flexibility. For those of you wondering how to start or change your fitness routine to match your desired results, here are some suggestions to point you in the right direction:

1. Weight Loss:

Weight train three times a week using high reps 15-20 for 3-4 sets with very little rest between sets. This will help by toning the muscles. Do cardio work like walking, running, cycling etc. starting with three times a week for 15-20 minutes at 60-70% of your maximal heart rate and slowly increase to 85% 3-5 times a week. You must also monitor your calorie intake to ensure it is up to 500 calories less per day than you expend in order to safely aim for a one-pound weight loss per week. See "Your Calorie Counting Calculation" on page 37.

2. Muscle Gain:

Train with resistance including machines and free weights 3-4 times a week. Increase the weight until you can only perform 3-4 sets with a maximum of 8-10 reps. The last rep of each set should be to muscle failure but with strict form. Rest about one minute between sets. See Chapter Four.

3. Strength:

This requires 3-5 sets using at least 80% of your "one rep maximum" (1RM) and dropping the reps to between 2-6. To determine your 1RM calculate (weight X reps X .03) + weight = your one rep max. Rest about two minutes between sets. See "Muscle Building Guidelines" on page 18.

4. Cardiovascular Efficiency:

Keep these in mind: Frequency, Intensity, Time and Type (F.I.T.T.). Slowly increase from 3 to 5 days a week. Elevate the maximum heart rate range from 60% to 85%. Gradually increase the time you are performing the cardio from 15 minutes up to 50 minutes. If it is not your goal to lose weight you must remember to increase your caloric intake to offset the expenditure of calories lost during the workout.

5. Flexibility:

Perform stretches 5-7 days a week regardless of whether you are working out that day. Always warm up with at least 5-7 minutes of light exercise or dynamic stretching. Stretch all the major muscle groups for two sets. Hold each stretch for 10-15 seconds at your own full range of motion, exhaling during the movement and avoiding bouncing movements.

Fitting SMART Fitness Goals into Your Program

When it comes to fitness, your program should fit your goals and what you need are SMART goals. The reason most attempts at fitness programs are short lived is not the fact that you can't achieve them; rather it's that you have set unrealistic goals that quickly become morale defeating. By setting SMART short and long-term goals you are more likely to stay committed. To beak it down SMART stands for Specific, Measurable, Attainable, Realistic and Time Targeted.

Take the time to plan your program, remembering that failing to plan is planning to fail. Let's address each facet of the SMART goals principal.

S   *Specific* :

Know what it is that you want to accomplish. To say: "I want to get fit" is too broad ranging and very difficult to assess. Ask yourself what needs improvement. Take the four main components of fitness and write out specific goals, be it body composition (lean muscle vs fat), increasing muscle (muscle mass, strength, power or endurance),cardiovascular improvement or flexibility.

M   *Measurable* :

How will you know when you've accomplished your goals? Clearly define your goals so you can recognize when you've reached them for both short-term and long-term. For all your goals make sure you note where you are now and where you want to be and chart your progress. For example: if it's cardiovascular fitness, check your heart rate beats per minute during your routine and chart it so that you can see the reduction as you progress.

A   *Attainable* :

Can you possibly reach your goals? If you decide you want to loose 50 pounds in a month you've set an unattainable goal. A SMART weight reduction goal would be one to two pounds a week, doing it sensibly and safely.

R   *Realistic* :

Is it likely you can do it? If you have a hectic schedule and you have set a goal of getting to the gym every day, you might want to re-think your goal. You might set a goal of getting to the gym 3 times a week for your short-term goal and re-asses it in a couple of months.

T   *Time Targeted* :

How long will this take and set a timetable. Getting those rock-hard, "six-pack abs" in two weeks is pressing the time target a bit. Most short-term goals should be time targeted for 8 weeks and long-term 6-12 months.

Consider your current fitness program or lifestyle and ask yourself: What worked in the past and what didn't work? What do you need to develop? Consider new and existing ideas and alternatives. What goals will you need to set in order to achieve the desired results? What behaviors need to change to support this direction? With these questions answered, or at least considered, start setting your SMART goals to stay committed. Perform all the components of the test again in eight weeks to monitor your progress.

Putting Your Best Foot Forward

Shoe manufacturers and athletes have been working closely with researchers over the last few decades. The result is advancements in design that contribute to improved safety. Shoes are built to support and absorb shock in the feet, ankles and the rest of the body in the areas that will be most affected during specific sports.

If you are a runner you should get proper running shoes. Good running shoes will have a well-padded soul to absorb and displace your weight from heel to toe. The force on your body created while running can be equal to three times your body weight on each impact. They should also have good tread to avoid slipping.

If aerobics classes are your thing you will be moving laterally a lot. This requires more ankle support and less tread to avoid catching on the floor and twisting an ankle or knee.

Indoor sports on smooth floors like basketball or lacrosse in which running and quick forward and lateral movements are involved, require high top shoes with great ankle support and smooth tread to avoid unexpected gripping on the floor.

Cross trainers are probably the way to go for most people who participate in several activities. They are, just as their name indicates, a cross between the other shoes. They are mid height at the ankle and have medium tread. These shoes would be perfect for normal gym use, lifting weights, working with stationary cardio equipment or even low impact body sculpt type group fitness classes.

For those of you who just like to go for a walk there are walking shoes. They have a low top, medium cushion on the souls and medium tread, which is ideal for shopping or walking to work.

Calculating Your Body Mass Index (BMI)

Have you ever been to a doctor's office and seen the height and weight charts and wondered where you fit in? As a society, we are obsessed with weight and ruled by the almighty scale. The body mass index scale is fairly simple to calculate and provides for a general guide to the benefits and risks associated with your weight as proportionate to your height.

Example : a 25-year-old
5'7" weighing 150 lbs

Step 1 : convert to metric
5'7" = 170 cm
150 lbs. = 68 kg

Step 2 : convert cm to meters
$170 \div 100 = 1.70$
then square it
$1.70 \times 1.70 = 2.89$

Step 3 : divide the weight by the height squared
$68 \div 2.89 = 23.5$

Body Mass Index is 23.5

As a *general guideline* consider the following. If your BMI is less than 20 you fall into the "underweight" category and may experience some health risks. If you fall between 20-25 BMI you are in the "normal" range. Those up to a 27 BMI could be slightly "overweight" and those over 30 could face considerable health risks such as diabetes, heart disease and problems with elevated blood pressure.

What the BMI does not take into consideration is the fact that muscle weighs more than fat. Therefore, a very muscular person can have a high BMI yet be in excellent physical condition and have little health risk. Conversely a person who lacks lean muscle and cardiovascular conditioning can have a BMI that falls into the normal range yet have considerable health risks due to their poor fitness level.

The point of this exercise is to make sure you consider your fitness and activity levels when determining if you need to lose or gain a few pounds.

Keeping a Fitness Journal

The beginning of a new year or the start of a new fitness program are perfect times to start keeping a fitness log or more accurately a journal.

A fitness journal will note times, speed and duration of cardio sessions or the pounds, sets and repetitions lifted in strength training. Your journal should go a couple of steps further and not be limited to the actual workout. It should include: short and long-term goals, eating, drinking (especially water), sleeping habits, and of course your workouts. You may be working out faithfully but failing to eat right, hydrate or get enough sleep. Without gathering all the information you may find yourself in a quandary as to why you aren't seeing results. You may need major changes in one area and minor subtle changes in another.

A complete journal will also raise your level of commitment and accountability. You will be able to more readily identify poor habits or patterns in your activity. Patterns in eating are usually the first thing that will leap out at you within the first month. You will likely notice certain meals will either increase or diminish the efficiency of your workout. Once you put pen to paper you are also more apt to be conscientious about

your water intake during exercise and on a daily basis.

Be sure to also include a reward system in your journal. Don't fall into the all work and no play syndrome. Most people will work harder if they know there is a light at the end of the tunnel. This is why, at the very least on a monthly basis, you should take time to enjoy a break. Miss a workout, eat a forbidden desert, sleep in or go out and buy some new clothes.

Another one of the biggest pitfalls is to record only either the good or the bad. Your journal should be as complete as possible with both the positive and the negative aspects.

Be careful how you measure or evaluate your successes. The most common measure in a fitness program is the weight scale, but try to only weigh yourself once a month. Use other means such as improved cardio endurance, more strength, having your clothes fit better or just plain feeling better, be your guide and be sure to note it. It doesn't all have to be empirical data. How you feel and how you feel about yourself are just as valuable information to include in your journal as the numbers on the scale.

Remember, write in your journal daily when it is fresh in your mind and be honest with your entries so as not to cheat yourself.

CHAPTER THREE

Warm-Up & Stretching

Warm-Up

The warm up portion of your exercise routine is very important and should not be bypassed. If you have ever jumped into a fitness class or into your workout and found the first couple of minutes of cardio or the first sets of resistance training made you feel out of breath you can appreciate the significance of the warm-up.

During the first few minutes of exercise your respiratory system is in a state of oxygen deficit and will fatigue quickly if not given an adequate opportunity to adjust to the workload. The warm up is necessary to gradually prepare the muscles, most importantly your heart, for the exercise ahead.

A proper warm-up can be as little as three minutes for an advanced athlete capable of understanding their body or can be ten minutes for beginners to ensure elevation of your heart rate by at least 40 beats per minute.

As an example, if your resting heart rate is 75 beats per minute your warm-up should bring it up to 115. This may seem high for some beginners who may find that their warm-up based on their resting heart rate will enter into their age predicted target cardio training zone. If this is the case you should seek professional guidance on preparing your workout.

The warm up can range from walking on a treadmill for new exercisers to more complex low intensity dynamic movements used as a rehearsal of the movements to be performed during your routine. For boxers and kickboxers, skipping and shadow boxing for a round or two is the perfect warm-up.

We all have good days and bad days, so too do we have high energy and low energy days. The warm-up gives us a chance to get our mental focus on the workout and some time to evaluate our energy level. If your energy feels high that day you may want to alter your workout to increase the intensity and if it's at the lower end of the scale, decrease the intensity accordingly.

Other than the increased heart beats per minute, you can assess your warm-up's effectiveness by observing physical changes to your body. Watch for your skin colour to get just a little reddish, your muscles should feel warmer, a little perspiration should appear and you should feel your breathing pattern increase slightly.

When you have warmed up successfully, decide whether you will stretch or continue into your cardio training zone. The deciding factor on that issue is: will stretching assist in the exercise I am about to do, such as kicking, or is it best to keep going and maintain the elevated heart rate? That is truly an individual decision as many fitness enthusiasts have done it both ways effectively.

Stretching 101

Stretching is probably one of the most neglected parts of fitness training and health in general.

Many people will take part in a fitness class, workout or work around the house and quickly move on to the next task because they are in a hurry to get going. By scurrying along you miss a very integral component of your overall fitness. Take five minutes prior to the activity to do some light cardio movement to slightly raise the body temperature before stretching.

Never stretch without a warm-up. Cold muscles are not pliable and you could cause slight tears to the muscles. Dynamic stretches (performed during a warm-up limiting the range of motion to about 75%) and mimicking the movements of the routine to be performed will allow the muscles to be more elastic in nature and prepared for the work ahead.

Whether it is aerobics, resistance/weight training, going for a walk or doing household chores you are repeatedly contracting the muscles. The heavier or more intense the activity the more contraction that is involved requiring not only the muscles, but also the connective tissue, tendons and ligaments to be shortened and stressed. Stretching restores the natural length to the muscles, tendons and ligaments and increases the range of motion to the joints. Greater range of motion reduces degeneration of the joints as well as the risk of injury due to tightness and inflexibility.

Intense physical activity causes a build up of lactic acid in the muscles that can result in soreness. Gradually stretching each body part worked for as little as 15-30 seconds is all it takes to relieve it.

As you stretch, never bounce or use a jerking motion. Slowly reach out elongating the muscles while exhaling and holding at a point of mild discomfort.

Most people associate stretching only with exercises, however, poor posture as a result of a sedentary lifestyle can be improved greatly with simple relaxation stretching at work or at home. Sitting for prolonged periods of time causes a shortening and tightening of the muscles in the legs, particularly the hamstrings and hips. Tightness in these areas can be directly linked to lower back pains.

Typical chores around the house like gardening, raking or the much-loved snow shoveling, should be accompanied by a short period of stretching before and after to thwart the onset of stiffness and soreness.

Stretch Your Quality of Life with Flexibility Training

There are many daily tasks that we take for granted like bending over to tie our shoes or reaching to the top shelf of the cupboard for our morning cereal. For some people this is difficult or impossible.

As we have a tendency to be a more sedentary population than past generations our bodies adapt to our lifestyle. All too often this results in poor posture and a significant reduction in our mobility. When you add in the inevitable aging process we have the increased likelihood of dependence due to self induced health problems.

Stretching and flexibility training can reverse the effects of the aging process and years of inactivity, therefore, improving your quality of life.

Some people have physical disabilities limiting their flexibility but for most it's just a product of inactivity and failing to realize the consequences and alternatives.

Four to seven days a week of gentle reaching, bending and stretching activities will help keep your muscles relaxed and joints mobile.

Stretching is essential to everyone just to remain functional, as well as those involved in exercise from the home fitness enthusiast to the competitive athlete. Flexibility will help prevent injuries and enhance sports performance and agility. For those involved in resistance or weight training it will allow for muscle growth by restoring the natural length to the muscles after contraction and prevent the lack of mobility commonly referred to as being muscle bound.

There are two basic types of stretching or flexibility training.

Dynamic stretching, which is used as a warm up to other training, and static stretching which is performed with warm muscles at the end of the training session or physical activity.

Dynamic stretching takes the muscles through a moderate range of motion in a rehearsal type movement. Think of it as though you were going to play baseball.

You wouldn't immediately try to throw the ball over the center field fence; you would play short toss and then increase the distance. This is the same principal as the dynamic stretch. Start slow and increase the speed to warm up the muscles around the joints.

Static stretching is done at the conclusion of the exercise and is a gradual lengthening of the muscles. Never stretch to your limit with cold muscles as they are not as pliable as they are when warmed up and strains and pulls can occur.

If you don't plan to workout but want to stretch take five to ten minutes to warm up first. The warm-up can be a short walk or a few times up and down the stairs at home. Stretch each of the major muscle groups and joints. Slowly stretch while exhaling and hold the stretch from 10-30 seconds, release, take a deep breath and perform the same stretch remembering not to bounce or hold your breath. Bouncing movements actually cause a natural reflex to contract the muscle to prevent over-lengthening and reduce full range of motion.

An entire full body stretching routine can be accomplished in as little as seven minutes a day.

CHAPTER FOUR

Resistance Training

Muscling Up

Weight loss and muscle toning are not the only reasons people take up weight or resistance training. Bodybuilding is a very popular sport and even if you don't plan to compete, it can be an immensely uplifting experience. Transforming and sculpting your body into an impressive physique can really boost your self-esteem.

A person's genetic structure is a prime factor in muscle building. Some males (and females) are blessed with naturally muscular body types. For these people muscle gains through proper training and nutrition are quick. For others, not so genetically gifted, hard work and diligence are the keys.

Lifting weights is only one of the three important parts of gaining muscle mass. The other two key ingredients, equally crucial to success, are rest and nutrition.

One of the most common mistakes is over training. The muscles grow while resting not while working out. When you lift weights you are causing microscopic tears to the muscles which, when properly fed and rested, will regenerate bigger and stronger. Exercising the same muscle groups each day will deter growth not enhance it. A rest period of 48-72 hours is needed for full recovery after a high intensity session.

In order to build mass and power the weight lifted must be sufficient to allow only 6-10 repetitions maximum for 3-4 sets. Merely increasing the weights without ensuring proper form creates the potential for injury. A term often used in weight training is the "one rep maximum" (1RM). To determine your 1RM without piling a ton of weight on the bar, try using the following equation: (weight X reps X .03) + weight = 1RM. Five reps or less is best for accuracy. As strength and size increase so will your 1RM. See "Muscle Building Guidelines" on page 18.

By practicing strict technique you will find that you use lighter weight than expected, increasing safety, and getting better results. Once you have carefully planned out the right weight, make sure your program is well balanced with specific exercises for all the body parts. When inexperienced lifters go for the show muscles like the biceps and chest they create muscle imbalance and lack of symmetry.

Finally, nutrition as in all fitness programs should include complex carbs for energy, protein for rebuilding muscle tissue and water for hydration to ensure the gains you want.

Don't Resist Resistance Training

Is resistance training really necessary if you are performing a regular cardio boxing or kickboxing program to burn off those unwanted pounds? To answer simply, yes. Cardio is necessary but should not be the only component of your fitness program.

There is a common misconception that you only burn off fat while you're sweating it out during your cardio session. Educating yourself as to the benefits of resistance training in pursuit of weight loss will help release you from the "cardio, cardio, and more cardio" state of mind. The body's ability to burn calories is enhanced by adding muscle. The newly developed muscle not only burns off fat at rest, it also has other positive effects such as increasing your metabolism and reducing or reversing the affects of osteoporosis.

- Your body burns off 35-50 more calories per day for every pound of lean muscle you add.
- A strength/resistance training program practiced three times a week increases your metabolism by 12% allowing you to consume up to 230 additional calories per day without increasing your present weight.
- Your metabolism can increase up to 73% by performing as little as 20 minutes of strength training one hour before having a meal.
- A regular resistance program alone can burn up to six pounds a year.
- Strength training can provide additional energy, increasing activity level by 27%, which in turn will eliminate more calories.
- Weight training three times a week increases the metabolism reducing harmful metabolic by-products.
- Working out with weights will improve your overall physique, create higher self-esteem and reduce incidences of anxiety.

Strength training reduces the loss of lean muscle mass due to aging. Between the ages of 20 and 75 the body can lose up to 30% of its lean muscle without some form of resistance exercise.

Resistance Training

Most people looking to get in shape consider resistance training, commonly referred to as weight training. Women often are afraid that if they lift weights they will become muscular and masculine in appearance. The physiological and hormonal differences between men and women will prevent this in most cases. Weight training for women increases muscle tone, strength and endurance. Resistance training for women will also assist in maintaining bone density and help reduce the incidence of osteoporosis.

There are a variety of possible training routines and equipment. There are machines that will isolate the muscles worked and add an element of safety. This is ideal for the beginner to get the muscles working and build confidence. Free weights incorporate balance and recruitment of other smaller muscle groups. Free body exercises, using only your own body weight, can also be very effective. Other equipment, like resistance tubing or exercise stability balls, can provide an excellent full body workout.

When starting out be sure to work all the major muscle groups beginning with the large multi-joint muscles and finishing with the smaller single joints.

Your workouts should be 2-3 times a week 45-60 minutes and include a warm up at the beginning and stretching at the end. Always stretch with warm muscles. This helps maintain your full range of motion and assists in the recovery phase. Muscles don't grow during the workout; they grow during rest. Proper rest between workouts will allow for better results and less incidence of injuries, strains and sore muscles.

Choose 8-10 exercises that include abs, legs, chest, back, shoulders, triceps and biceps in that order. Keep the sets from 1-3 as a beginner and increase to 3-5 sets as you advance. If your goal is muscle endurance and toning complete 12-15 reps per set using light weight. If your goal is strength and muscle building perform 8-10 reps with heavy weight. The last rep being the last you can complete with ***proper form***. Remember to never give up proper form just to put more weight on the bar.

As a beginner it is easy to get excited when you see your biceps muscle growing or those thighs firming up, but be sure to stick to your program and don't over-train as it will reverse the positive effects.

Train smart, train safe and include cardiovascular work for lifelong health.

Super-Sets for Fitness

Ever notice when you go through a fast food drive-thru that the friendly, often garbled, voice at the other end of the speaker will ask: "Would you like to Super-Size that order"? Sure you have, and it's okay to admit you go to fast food restaurants, unless of course it's every day. If you Super-Size your meals on wheels why not Super-Size your weight training program with Super-Sets?

Very few other types of weight or resistance training can test your limits as much as Super-Set training. Super-Sets will increase your enthusiasm for training while improving specific aspects of your fitness. Initially, you'll enjoy incorporating Super-Sets because they provide variety and challenge from your usual training regiment. After experimenting with them, you'll want to use Super-Set sessions with regularity because of the way they help motivate you to train with better results.

Super-Sets are a series of reps and sets of exercises, which are carried out without any recovery time and with decreasing intensity. Super-Sets can be an amazing training routine when you are striving for strength and endurance. Using as little as 10 seconds rest can be enough recovery time to restore your body to almost maximum intensity. It is therefore possible to repeat a large number of proper form/technique sets and reps of exercises without incurring a lot of recovery time.

You will be shocked with the quick increase in strength you will gain by incorporating Super-Sets in your training. Try performing a Super-Set of bench presses starting off by pressing an extremely heavy weight, close to your "one rep maximum" (1RM). See "Muscle Building Guidelines" on page 18. When you reach the point of failure, have your training partner remove just enough weight from the barbell so that you can continue lifting. When you are exhausted again, your partner takes off just enough weight so that you can keep lifting. Continue in this pattern of lifting to failure, reducing the resistance by taking off weight, again lifting to failure, until the only thing left in your hands is the bar. This same principle can be used with any exercise, such as bicep curls, flyes, etc.

Train smart and train safe, always have a training partner for Super-Sets.

Muscle Building Guidelines

Many people fight a never-ending battle to shed those excess pounds and trim up. With weight loss issues being so prevalent, there is a great deal of coverage in magazines, books, Internet and media in general on how to lose weight but not as much information on how to gain weight, or to be specific, gain muscle. The person looking to gain a few pounds must consume the right balance of calories, combining carbs and protein, while adopting a muscle building type routine.

Here are some tips for designing your own weight training routine to pack on some pounds of solid muscle. In order to gain muscle growth, which is called hypertrophy, you must be training at an intensity of 70-80% of your one repetition maximum. The one rep max, also referred to as 1RM, is important to determine for all weight lifting programs and especially for muscle building routines. For each exercise you are planning to include in your program use the following formula: Weight you are lifting X Repetitions X .03 + Weight lifted = Your One Rep Max. To get the best and most accurate determination of the one repetition maximum use enough weight to keep the reps to five or less.

For example, if you plan to incorporate the bench press into your routine, and if you put 100 pounds on the bar and can lift it 5 times with the 5th rep being the last you can do with proper form, then you take those figures and plug them into the formula: 100 (Weight you are lifting) X 5 (The reps) X .03 + 100 (Weight lifted) = 115 pounds (your 1RM). Now multiply that number (115 pounds) by 70%, which works out to be 81 pounds and then by 80%, which is 92 pounds. Round off to 80-95 pounds, which is the weight you should be using to effectively create a weight/resistance program to build muscle. Once you have established the proper weight for each exercise you are ready to start.

Set up a program that allows for 3-4 training sessions a week, with 2-4 sets of 8-10 repetitions. Keep the routine to basic or compound exercises that use more than one muscle group at a time and ensure that you have a balanced full body workout. Don't get caught in the trap of concentrating on the show muscles like biceps or chest. Some basic exercises that provide for a great overall workout include: squats, calf raises, bench press, overhead press, bent arm row, bicep curls and tricep curls.

Good luck with your muscling up.

Fitness Circuit Training Routine

In a traditional strength training program a variety of exercises are preformed with the desired result being toning, muscle building or power. Generally 2-3 sets are done with rests of 30-90 seconds between and then repeating the same exercise. This is done to give the muscle group worked rest and time for the lactic acid to subside before using them again.

During spring and summer most people want to get their workout done quickly

without sacrificing efficiency, safety or results. If you belong to a fitness club or have a home gym you can drastically reduce your non-productive waiting/recuperating time by incorporating a circuit training routine. If you have a trainer at your club have him or her prepare a personalized workout based on your goals with the equipment available. By arranging your exercises in such an order that you can move from one muscle group to the next you can avoid waiting and therefore condense the workout time.

There are several types of programs based on this system. You can switch between upper and lower body muscle groups or between pushing and pulling muscle group exercises.

The following routine can be done 2-3 times a week and should be in conjunction with a cardio routine 3-4 times a week in the target heart range for 20-30 minutes. See "Calculating Your Target Heart Rate Training Zone" on page 6.

Circuit Training Routine

- Warm up with cardio in target heart range
- Use the workout chart to record your exercises, weights and reps
- If possible perform the exercises in the order listed below
- Do reps for one minute ensuring proper technique and slow controlled movement

- Immediately move to the next exercise with the only rest to set up; this will save time and keep your heart rate elevated
- At the conclusion of the circuit stretch each muscle group
- Repeat circuit

1. Sit-Ups/Crunches, Floor or With Ball (Abs)
2. Bench Press (Pectorals/Chest)
3. Leg Extensions (Quadriceps)
4. Pec-Flyes (Outer Pectorals)
5. Leg Press or Squats (Quads, Hamstrings & Glutes)
6. Lat-Pulldowns (Lats/Back)
7. Calf Raises (Calves & Ankles)
8. Shoulder Press (Deltoids/Shoulders)
9. Tricep Pushdowns (Triceps)
10. Bicep Curls (Biceps)

Smart Fitness Tips for Dumbbells

Anyone starting out on a resistance/weight training program is wise to use home gyms and machines at the gym as they ensure proper technique and reduce the risk of injury by dropping weights.

As you progress you may want to advance to dumbbells, incorporating an element of balance and increased range of motion. It also provides for a more unique workout that the machines won't allow. If your fitness club has a full set of dumbbells you've got it made. If not and you plan on exercising at home there are two types of dumbbells to consider: a dumbbell set that comes with two hand bars, collars and plates; or fixed dumbbells. The dumbbells with interchangeable plates are fine but

invariably a collar will come loose and when one of the plates lands on you it usually leaves a mark, and not just on the floor! Fixed weights are just that, fixed at certain poundage and secured on the handle.

Build your collection by starting out with a few sets of dumbbells of various weights. Keep them light and keep adding weight to your dumbbell rack as you progress.

A workout bench that can be adjusted from flat to 45 and 90 degrees is a bonus but can be pricy. An anti-burst stability ball can be used in place of a bench and can be a useful tool when it comes to abdominal and back exercises, not to mention the increased degree of balance. One draw back when using dumbbells is that if you're not careful the floor can take a beating and get marked up. Some inexpensive rubber floor matting can prevent this and also reduce the noise.

Exercising with dumbbells doesn't change the usual resistance training principles. Toning requires 2-3 sets of lighter weights with 12-15 repetitions. Building strength and mass requires 2-3 sets of 8-10 reps with heavier poundage.

Get on the Ball and Get Fit

One of the most popular pieces of fitness equipment is the exercise stability ball. The stability ball was used in Europe for many years in the medical profession to treat back injuries by increasing core strength. About 40 years ago physical therapists in North America began using the stability ball with patients requiring strength and flexibility in the lower back. In the early 1990's the idea of the stability ball emerged from the rehabilitation field to be utilized as an effective tool for fitness training. They can be found in almost every gym in North America and are fast finding a place in most households.

Studies have shown that 80% of adults over the age of 25 will experience some degree of lower back pain. The solution is to strengthen the lower back by increasing the core strength before the back weakens or to improve your back health if you are already experiencing lower back discomfort. The core trunk area includes the back and the abdominal muscles. Improvement in the functional fitness of older adults has been achieved with as little as two hours a week of training on the ball. The stability ball can replace the traditional exercise bench and add an element of balance and coordination to your workout. The abs, back and trunk are used as stabilizing muscles, meaning that they are worked to some degree on almost every exercise.

Slight changes in body positioning on the ball can either increase the intensity for more advance persons or reduce it for the beginner. Women in the early stages of pregnancy can benefit by working out on the ball to strengthen the lower back to alleviate the incidence of muscle strains and soreness in the later trimesters. As the baby grows, so does the resistance. The muscles will slowly adapt to the increase in weight in the same way you would progressively increase weight in a traditional resistance-training program.

The ball also provides a greater range of motion for flexibility stretches while supporting the trunk and spinal column.

Start with a light warm-up using slow full body movements including all the major muscles and joints. See Chapter Three.

Perform each of the following exercises 1-3 times, 8-12 reps.

1. Abdominals:

Sit on the ball and walk your feet forward until you have the ball in the small of your back. Place your hands behind your head, allow your back to lower backward over the ball until you are parallel to the floor, then contract the stomach muscles and sit up.

Lie flat on the floor on your back, ball in your hands with arms and legs extended straight out. Bring your hands and feet up at the same time in a "jack-knife" movement and catch the ball between your feet and lower it to the floor. Repeat the exercise transferring the ball back and forth from hands to feet.

2. Lower Back:

Lie flat on the floor on your back, legs extended straight out with your heels resting on the ball, arms on the floor out to your side for balance. Tighten the glutes (buttocks) and abs to raise your hips off the floor until your body is straight, lower slowly to the floor and repeat.

Lie over the ball facing down with the ball under the tummy-hips area, extend both legs and arms straight out touching the floor as your points of balance. Raise your right arm and left leg at the same time as high as you can then lower and alternate with the left arm and right leg.

3. Legs :

Place the ball against the wall, turn your back and lean against it with it in the small of your back. Walk your feet forward slightly so that you are leaning your weight against the ball. Keeping your back straight and head up squat down bringing the bottom of your thighs parallel to the ground then straighten your legs pushing yourself back up into the semi-standing position. Try different positions like feet together, shoulder width apart or one legged lunges with one foot forward and one foot back, toe to the floor for balance. Each exercise works slightly different muscles.

4. Chest and Arms :

Kneel with the ball in front of you against your thighs, lean forward over the ball with your hands on the floor walk yourself forward. The farther you move forward, keeping the upper body parallel to the floor, the more of your body weight you are supporting. From there perform push-ups coming down as close to the floor as possible and back up.

Pilates + Stability Ball = Results

The fitness world has gone through many recent changes. The most popular programs involve Pilates and stability ball training. Most people think that these are new breakthroughs and are either interested in getting involved or skeptical about their results or effectiveness. Actually, neither of these programs is new.

Pilates was the brainchild of a man named Joseph Pilates who created his own style of exercises in the 1920's based on slow continuous movement through full range of motion. The goal is to create functionally developed muscles that are lean and long. With no rest between sets you can use very light or no weights to be effective. This routine is similar to yoga and can result in tremendous increases in endurance, strength and flexibility. The isometric contraction of the muscles allows the participant to increase the intensity without adding weights. This also decreases the incidence of strains to the muscles, joints, tendons and ligaments.

Controlled breathing techniques, concentration on proper posture, and core strength with recruitment of the abdominal muscles are features that are also found to be the fundamental basis for the stability ball program.

The stability ball is not new either. It was created in Europe in the 1950's and brought to North America in the 60's by those in the physiotherapy profession. By the 1990's the effectiveness of the ball training with rehabilitative injury programs lent itself to mainstream fitness. With the emphasis on core strength involving the abdominals and back it fills a need in our sedentary society. The majority of these back problems are as a result of lack of exercise and poor posture. The stability ball provides an element of balance, coordination and agility combined with strength and flexibility. See the article titled: "Get on the Ball and Get Fit" on page 20.

Both Pilates and stability ball training can be done by anyone of any age or fitness level. The participant is in complete control of the intensity and can modify it to suit their needs or limitations.

The perfect combination is Pilates on the Ball. All aspects of both disciplines are combined taking the most popular and effective exercises and incorporating them for a full body workout that can revolutionize your current program.

Medicine Ball Training

In the 1940's and 50's medicine balls were common pieces of equipment in all gyms. In an effort to modernize fitness equipment and programs technology has, in some cases, taken us away from proven methods. Fortunately fitness research and studies have brought back medicine ball training.

The medicine ball is a common tool used by personal trainers. Medicine ball training provides sport-specific as well as general strength throughout the body to establish balance and coordination to protect your core (abs and back) muscles and connective tissues from reaction movements and impacts. Whether you are playing baseball and reach for a sharply hit line drive or are playing hockey and take a body check, training to be fit for the unstable conditions will make you more likely to handle the stress of such a movement.

The medicine ball is not only useful to athletes, the benefit of strength-balance training can make daily tasks easier and safer. How many people strain muscles as their dog unexpectedly tugs on the leash, reaching to grab a bowl falling off the kitchen counter or unloading groceries from the car trunk? Exercises involving lifting, tossing and catching a medicine ball from a moving, standing or seated position can vastly increase strength and balance as well as reduce incidence of injury.

Medicine balls come in various weights, sizes and material. They usually range from 1 kilogram (2.2 pounds) to 7 kilogram (15.4 pounds) and 6" to 10" in diameter. If you are a beginner you should start with no heavier than a 3 kg ball and work your way up. You will be shocked how heavy it is when tossed to you or when it comes flying back at you when thrown against a wall.

Older style medicine balls are made of leather and are non-bouncing. The drawback of these models is that the surface becomes difficult to grip when your hands become sweaty and usually requires a partner to train and toss with. Most new balls are constructed of thick rubber and a textured surface ensuring a much safer grip. The rubber medicine balls also come in non-bouncing and bouncing types. The non-bouncing type will bounce slightly because of the rubberized surface but usually requires a partner to train and toss with. The bouncing variety, which can also be inflated or deflated slightly to your preference, can be used alone and bounced off the wall and floor for a great solo workout.

So take your medicine (ball) and stay healthy.

CHAPTER FIVE

Cardio Training

....

Heart Health

Your heart is the most important muscle in your body. Studies have shown tremendous health benefits with as little as two cardiovascular workouts a week. Your heart will become much more efficient making daily functions like walking up a flight of stairs much easier. Other less obvious benefits include normalizing your blood pressure while lowering your resting heart rate and reducing the likelihood of associated heart disease.

Your choice of cardio activities should involve the large muscle groups and can range from a brisk walk, stationary biking, treadmill, fitness or aerobic classes to interval and cross training.

The general recommendation for cardio-training is 3-7 times a week at 50-85% of the person's maximal oxygen intake or 60-90% of the age-predicted heart rate maximum. The reality of daily living and busy personal lives will not afford most people with the time for seven sessions a week. Keeping your personal schedule and goals in mind, try to aim for a minimum of two cardiovascular training sessions a week. On non-training days, this could be accomplished with an after dinner walk through the neighborhood. Less fit individuals should start with a cardiovascular training routine limiting it to 2-3 times a week for at least 20-30 minutes in the target heart rate training zone. If 20-30 minutes of continuous activity is too difficult at first it can be broken down into 10-minute segments without loosing much benefit. Starting off slow will lessen the likelihood of overstressing your heart and reduce the incidence of injury, strains and muscle soreness that will turn you off exercising. More active or experienced fitness enthusiasts will want to challenge themselves to achieve maximum benefits by increasing to 4-6 times a week for 20-60 minutes.

See "Calculating Your Target Heart Rate Training Zone" on page 6.

Training the Right Energy

Boxing and kickboxing both primarily involve the use of the anaerobic energy systems. When you start training think about the sport and the demands it puts upon your cardiovascular system.

For many years coaches and trainers would have the athletes running miles at a time without water breaks to get the legs and lungs in shape.

Great in theory. . .wrong in practice. Think about it, in both boxing and kickboxing, neither one requires the participant to run at a constant pace for 20, 30 or 40 minutes. They require short bursts of speed and then a slower pace or even a rest, like in a two or three minute round followed by a 30-60 second rest period. Train the body the way you intend to use it.

There are two energy systems in the human body, Anaerobic and Aerobic. Anaerobic is defined as "energy produced in absence of oxygen". This system is divided into two sub systems, the ATP-CP phosphagen system and the Fats Glycolysis system. ATP-CP phosphagen system activates when the muscle contractions are performed so quickly that the cardiovascular system can't keep up with the oxygen demands of the muscles. This system usually last for up to 30 seconds like short flurries of punches and kicks in a competitive bout. The Fast Glycolysis system then kicks in to try to produce more ATP-CP. The production of lactic acid, which is the burning sensation you get in the muscle, usually prevents you from continuing beyond two minutes like a round in boxing or kickboxing.

The aerobic system is broken into two sub-systems as well, Slow Glycolysis and Fat Oxidation. Both these systems rely on oxygen and are used for long duration, slow to moderate cardio work like long distance running or aerobics classes. Slow Glycolysis can last up to about two hours until it depletes the glucose from your body at which point the body's fat becomes the prime source of fuel to keep the body moving again like in long distance running or marathon swimming for many hours of continuous activity.

Now, back to boxing and kickboxing. It's not to say that long distance running isn't beneficial to your fitness and weight loss goals, but, if you are running long distances or long durations, you aren't preparing the anaerobic system used during the match. Train with sprints followed by either rest or slow active rest to allow the body to adjust, improve and develop quicker production within the ATP-PC system. This means less rest will be required to enable you to go all out again. Aside from sprints, stair climbs, agility circuits involving pylons and mini-hurdles will drastically affect your body in a positive way to perform at competition time.

Train smart by training the right energy system!

Running for Fitness

Running, although an excellent form of fitness training, can be very hard on your body, especially the feet, ankles, knees and hips if not performed properly. Before starting a running program you may want to attend a running clinic to gain valuable tips ensuring a safe and efficient fitness experience.

Beginners should start week one by jogging for 1 minute then walking for 1; X 10 for a total of 20 minutes. Week two: jog for 2 minutes and walk for 1; X 8, for a total duration of 24 minutes. Week three: the same but increase the reps to 9 and the duration to 27 minutes. The fourth week: jog for 3 minutes and walk for 1; X 8 for a total duration of 32 minutes.

Training with a group provides extra motivation and the additional benefit of safety in numbers and the advantage of gleaning tips from more experienced runners. Other essentials for running include proper footwear, a hat on sunny days and appropriate clothing made of polypropylene, not cotton.

Learning proper foot placement, landing gently heel to toe, will reduce the impact on your joints. Your stride should not be too long as it causes tightening of the hamstrings. A shorter stride will increase your speed. When it comes to form stay upright, chest forward, hips forward and swing your arms naturally to expend less energy.

Some people are reluctant to start a running program, fearing that it is a race and they don't want to finish last. You must keep in mind that if you are running for your own health and fitness benefits you are only competing against yourself.

Walking Your Way to Fitness

Many people interested in starting a fitness program voice concerns about not wanting to be stuck indoors. They don't want to buy expensive equipment or feel they are in too poor of shape to jump into a rigorous exercise routine. For those of you in these categories, walking may be just the thing for you. Brisk walking can be more beneficial than jogging or running as it produces less impact and strain on your joints and ligaments.

Studies indicate that regular brisk walking 3-5 times a week for 30 minutes will:

- Increase your metabolism to reduce weight.

- Lower your LDL (bad cholesterol) and increase you HDL (good cholesterol) to improve overall cholesterol levels.

- Assist in control of diabetes.

- Lower your blood pressure and improve overall heart health.

- Help improve your posture and reduce lower back pain.

- Release endorphins to help reduce stress and depression.

You will want to wear comfortable clothing suited for the weather. Walking isn't restricted to fair weather or only as a summer activity. However, during the summer months hydration is an especially important issue. Always carry a bottle of water with you and on extremely hot or sunny days don't forget to wear a hat and apply sunscreen. See "Helpful Hydration Hints" on page 35.

Proper fitting walking shoes are a must to prevent injuries ranging from blisters to shin splints. If you are just starting off, remember, there is no need to push yourself to the point of exhaustion to gain fitness benefit. The "Talk Test", which means being able to talk comfortably while walking and keeping your heart rate in the target range, should be your guide. See "Calculating Your Target Heart Rate Training Zone" on page 6.

For motivation and safety try to find a walking partner and keep a journal. A walking journal will give you a benchmark indicating where you started and how you have progressed. You can log the distance travelled in miles or kilometers or the time you walked in minutes. You can keep track of increased distance covered in the same time or, as your endurance improves, walk farther and faster.

You can also get a pedometer. A pedometer is a small device about the size of a pager and usually attaches to your belt. It counts each step you take and adds a real empirical element to your walking and journal keeping.

CHAPTER SIX

Abdominals

Flat Abs on Time

Some of the most common questions about exercise focus on the abdominal muscles, usually referred to as "abs".

Breaking the exercises down to work the four basic parts of the abs which are the upper, lower and obliques (both sides - love handle area), you will get the best results in the shortest time. By switching from muscle group to muscle group you do not need to waste time resting between exercises. Beginners should aim for three minutes to start and work up to 10 minutes repeating the circuit as necessary. Set your watch to signal every 30 seconds to change exercises. If you want to get really elaborate you can prepare yourself a tape or CD of motivational music that changes every 30 seconds. Try the following exercises doing as many as you can for 30 seconds and then switching to the next exercise. If you can't keep going for the 30 seconds, stop, relax and wait for the next exercise.

Semi-Crunch (upper abs): Lie flat on your back with your legs straight, heels on the ground and arms folded across your chest. Being careful not to arch your lower back, raise your torso 6-8 inches off the floor, keeping the lower body stationary then return to the starting position.

Feet to the Ceiling (lower abs): Lie on your back, hands at your sides or under your buttocks. Move through the following: legs bent and pulled toward the chest; legs extended in a pushing motion up to the ceiling; legs bent and pulled toward the chest again.

Crossover Twist-Crunches

(obliques): Lie on your back with your knees bent, cross your left knee over the right keeping your right foot flat on the floor. With your hands behind your head, raise your shoulders off the ground and twist toward your left knee touching it with your right elbow. Lower to the starting position and repeat. For the next 30 seconds change foot position and twist-crunch to your right knee.

The Plank (entire abdominal & core area): Get into a pushup position, except your body weight should be resting on your forearms instead of your hands. Push your body to a position parallel to the floor tightening your stomach. Don't allow your back to arch and keep your shoulders, back, buttocks, and heels in a straight line. Hold for 30 or 60 seconds

Feel free to mix it up and add some of your favorites.

Abs

The following exercises are performed without rest between sets starting with as few as 10 reps and work up to 25-30 of each. Be sure to keep the movement slow and controlled while exhaling during contraction of the stomach muscles.

Upper Abs Half-Crunch : Lie flat on the floor, cross your feet and pull your knees up so that your thighs are straight up 90 degrees from the floor. Place your finger tips at your temple, (do not pull on your neck), without moving your legs maintaining the 90 degree position, raise your shoulders off the floor 4-6 inches, and repeat, keeping constant contraction on the ab muscles.

Heel to Toe : Extend both legs straight out placing your left heel on top of the right toe. With your hands in the same position as above repeat by raising your shoulders off the floor 4-6 inches keeping constant contraction on the ab muscles. Switch and put you right heel on your left toe.

Toe Tappers : Still lying flat on your back, legs up 90 degrees from the floor with your feet shoulder width apart. Hands are again at the temples. Drop both feet to the floor and instantly, as they touch in a sort of a toe tap movement, pull your legs back up as you crunch up your upper body lightly touching your elbows to the knees, and repeat. Remember the toes just lightly tap the floor and immediately come back up.

Back Bridges : For proper muscular balance, don't neglect the back muscles. While you are on your back, with your abs burning by now, place your feet down on the floor in a normal sit-up position and raise your hips up off the floor so that your shoulders are your upper base and your body is in a straight position from the knees to the shoulders on a 45 degree angle.

Alternate Back Extension : Lie in a face down position and extend your arms directly out above your head. Raise your right hand and left leg simultaneously and alternate to the left hand right leg working the lower back area.

More Ab Work

Good old fashion crunches are a great exercise but if you need to turn up the intensity you may want to try adding some resistance and lowering the reps.

Lie down on the floor with your knees bent 45 degrees with the soles of your feet flat on the floor. Take a dumbbell or weight plate and position the weight on the centre of your chest and try to perform 15 repetitions with good form. Use slow deliberate, controlled movement being sure to exhale as you come up, and inhale as you lower to the floor. Imagine that you are trying to pull your belly button in towards your spine and tighten your glutes at the same time on each rep.

You don't have to come all the way up bringing your shoulders up to your knees. Just raise your shoulders 3-4 inches off the floor and as you lower your shoulders down don't allow them to touch the floor. By not touching the floor you keep the ab muscles constantly engaged and increase the intensity. If you can't perform 15 reps, you have too much weight.

Once you have found the perfect weight, each week add 10% more, while maintaining 15 reps with strict form. For variation lie flat on the floor with your legs extended, calves flat on the floor and toes pointed to the ceiling.

CHAPTER SEVEN

Boxing & Kickboxing

Fitting Martial Arts into Fitness Training

Many people shy away from martial arts training because it is perceived as a fighting sport and not contributing to an overall true cardiovascular and resistance type workout. This is not the case and there are many different styles of martial arts with each enhancing your fitness program.

Let's separate what is and is not martial arts. Most fitness clubs offer classes like Tae Bo, Aerobic Kickboxing, Cardio-Karate or some form of aerobics class incorporating punches and kicks. These classes are aerobics classes and, although they are a good cardio workout, they are ***not*** martial arts training. Often they are taught by aerobics instructors with no experience in martial arts, therefore, the punches, blocks, kicks and combinations have little or no self-defence benefit and can leave the participants with a false sense of security that they have learned a skill to protect themselves against an attack. Martial arts prepares a person to defend themselves while increasing physical attributes such as cardiovascular endurance, flexibility, strength, coordination and agility, in addition to increasing self-confidence and self-esteem with an element of internal training.

Anyone who has participated in a typical martial arts class is well aware that abdominal training is an integral part. The prime source of power in martial arts comes from the core area of the body and focuses on proper breathing techniques.

All good fitness programs include short-term and long-term goals. Martial arts have a built in goal setting plan through the use of a belt grading system. Some people are turned off by the thought of belt grading but soon appreciate it as a way to recognize personal accomplishments and motivate for further progress.

Kickboxing emphasizes an intense cardiovascular workout combining the proper punching techniques of boxing and kicks from martial arts. Karate and taekwondo add a dimension of mental and physical discipline while emphasizing balance, flexibility and full range of motion to deliver powerful strikes and kicks. Progressing through a belt ranking system, participating in in-house club events, tournaments, sparring, kata and other demonstrations provide ample venue to challenge you and measure your skill and fitness level.

Like boxing classes, that have become immensely popular, fitness kickboxing offers the opportunity to train like a real kickboxer, gaining all the benefits without having to get in the ring. Studies have revealed that a 45-60 minute kickboxing class can burn off 600-800 calories. In addition to the weight loss, you are building lean muscle, which raises your metabolism burning calories at rest and toning the whole body. The kicking exercises concentrate on the thighs, hips and buttocks unlike any other workout.

By utilizing partner training you get the increased motivation and commitment that makes it ideal for couples wanting to workout together or regular training partners of any age or fitness level. Unlike traditional aerobics classes where everyone is staying at the same pace, your intensity is determined by you and your partner.

The use of focus pads and heavy bags provide a tremendous form of resistance training that builds lean muscle and has the added bonus helping to increase bone density.

The Punch and Kick Workout

People often ask how to vary their program to get a full body cardio/resistance workout in the shortest time. Incorporating a heavy bag routine into your fitness regiment can provide cardio and resistance training all in one 30-minute workout with the extra perk of abdominal work build right in.

"Heavy bags" or "punching bags" are relatively inexpensive and don't take up a lot of space; most gyms are now equipped with them. Punching and kicking against the weight of the bag provides excellent resistance to build lean muscle and bone density. The constant quick hands and arms motions combined with the footwork gets the heart pumping for an intense cardio session.

Since a lot of the punch and kick power comes from your abdominal muscles you will be working them on every strike. The abs act as a stabilizer for body movement, the rectus abdominus (front of the stomach) and the obliques (sides) are in constant use when punching and kicking. Uppercuts, hooks and roundhouse kicks emphasize the ab muscles in particular. Uppercuts and hooks can be thrown with the front or rear hand. With the uppercut, concentrate on bringing the elbow back to the rib cage area and drive the punch straight up turning the fist so that the palm is facing you. The hook is difficult to master but you want to keep the line from the elbow to the fist horizontal and do not bend at the wrist.

Some effective yet easy combinations to start with are: the left uppercut & right hook, the right uppercut & left hook, alternate hand uppercuts or hooks. Throw in some jabs (lead hand) and some crosses (rear hand) and mix it up. Get in close to the heavy bag, you can even lean into it a bit, stay crouched, feet shoulder width apart, use short punches and avoid swinging or flailing the arms.

Exhale and tighten the abs on each punch concentrating on bringing the power from the ab muscles, hips and legs. When it comes to roundhouse kicks, they can be thrown off the front or rear foot. Start by raising the kicking leg, pivot on the base foot while pointing the knee to the target, quickly extend the lower part of the leg and foot being sure to contract the abs and thrust the hip forward striking the bag with the top part of the foot (on the laces of your shoe). Retract quickly bringing it back to your fighting position.

Start your program with three 2-3 minute rounds with 30-60 seconds rests between rounds for water. Work your way up to 6-10 rounds.

CHAPTER EIGHT

Fitness for Any Age

Fitness Over 40

The old saying: "you're as young as you feel" is a great philosophy but your lungs, legs, arms and joints may not agree. The fact is, you can slow the aging process with exercise but you can't stop it. However, you can still workout at a high intensity level, as many people train and excel well into their 40's, 50's and beyond.

Before choosing a fitness activity you should first consider other aspects such as previous exercise history, weight, flexibility and genetics. Certain physical training is more beneficial to people over 40. Males are at a higher risk of cardiovascular disease over the age of 40 and women are more susceptible to osteoporosis. Women traditionally prefer aerobics classes and men generally prefer weight training. What might be best at this stage of life is some cross-training.

The metabolism slows down 10-15% as we reach middle age and exercise, in particular resistance training, will help maintain lean muscle mass to keep the fat burning metabolism revved up. It is important to remember that overtraining isn't the answer either. Training for more than five hours on a structured program will actually reduce the effectiveness and lead to other problems like over-use strains, sprains, tendonitis and even minute fractures. Over-training at 25 years old isn't good, overtraining at 45 years of age is even worse because it can take a prolonged period of time to rejuvenate.

Staying physically active every day and eating right are the keys to good health, longevity and maintaining quality of life. If you have a program you really enjoy, stick to it.

For variety you might want to try some of the following: stability ball training for strength, balance and development of the abdominals and lower back; yoga and Pilates for strength and flexibility; and bike riding, walking or running for cardiovascular and heart related benefits.

If you really feel energetic try a boxing or kickboxing class for a full body blast.

Older Adult Fitness Tips

With the advent of computers and hi-tech, hi-speed everything we, as humans, have actually slowed down compared to previous generations. Lack of physical exercise for some has reduced the ability to enjoy any spare time available. Others have recognized the need for regular physical activity to restore and maintain functional ability to continue independence.

The cruel reality of the aging process is that, unattended, there are noticeable changes to all components of fitness. Body composition will change and is usually accompanied by some extra, unwanted pounds. Reduced flexibility sets in as a result of years of poor posture. Strength diminishes in men, and women can experience osteoporosis as bone density decreases. Cardiovascular disease is prominent in men over 40 years of age and afflicts women over 50.

Here are some tips to reduce or perhaps even reverse some of the negative affects of aging:

- Consult your physician as to your current state of health and set realistic goals for the improvements you want to make.

- Stay active for at least 30 minutes each day. This includes tasks such as housekeeping, shopping, cutting the lawn, etc.

- Join clubs like bowling, golf and skiing, or recreational team sports such as men's slo-pitch and ladies' three pitch leagues.

- Make friendships with others who want to stay active. This will provide you with a support network and keep you committed.

- Try different activities that you enjoy. If you enjoy it you are more likely to stick with the program and see results.

- Check out the local Health, Wellness and Fitness Centres and evaluate the programs offered.

- If you have been exercising with a traditional program switch to a functional program. Functional means exercises that represent daily activities like walking or stair climbing.

- Concentrate on agility, balance and coordination exercises like Pilates, yoga, tai chi or stability ball routines. These routines are slower, involving less impact but at the same time provide elements of strength and flexibility that can be modified easily to meet your fitness level.

- Lastly, be sure to reward yourself for your accomplishments and don't be too hard on yourself if you temporarily falter.

Physical Activity for Children and Youth

Today's youth have become increasingly less active than those of past generations. Some elementary school children receive as little as two physical education classes a week. Now, before we jump on the teachers or the local school board, we must realize there is only so much time and gym space available to be shared.

The responsibility to keep kids active must shift back to the parents. To say: "That's what the teachers get paid for" doesn't help the situation.

Currently most school programs involve such activities as floor hockey, football, soccer, basketball, gymnastics, badminton, volleyball and various track and field events. All of which are excellent sources of exercise and team building skills. The problem is that it isn't quite enough. Some children will want to stay active and be outside after school every day playing road hockey, soccer, skipping our just running around playing tag. Others may need a little encouragement to get away from the computer or off the couch glued to the TV.

There is nothing wrong with allowing children to spend time on the computer, playing video games and watching television. These are all activities that can promote learning, entertain and are a necessity in the peer group hierarchy of needs. What is needed is a healthy balance between mental and physical activities.

Health Canada has released a physical activity guide for children and youth. The three areas of concern addressed in the guide are: Endurance, Flexibility and Strength. Put very simply for children to understand they are as follows:

Endurance activities make you breathe deeper, your heart beat faster and warm up your body.

Flexibility activities are things like bending, stretching and reaching that keep your joints moving.

Strength activities build your muscles and bones.

The guide also provides a suggested timetable to increase physical activity and reduce inactivity. It's easy to follow and can serve as a sort of goal setting game for the kids.

Make it fun and interesting by sharing in the experience with your kids and even setting up a little reward system to provide motivation.

The idea is to start slow with 20 minutes of moderate activity daily and 10 minutes of vigorous activity. By increasing moderate activity (walking, biking, playing outdoors, etc.) by 10 minutes a day and vigorous activity (running, soccer, etc.) by five minutes a day, you will have gained 90 minutes of physical activity a day after six months.

Active children will become active adults.

Youth Sports Training = Training for Life

Sports can be a very positive influence on youth development in both the physical and mental aspects. Unfortunately they can also be a very unpleasant experience for some children. The child that is always picked last for a schoolyard team, or sits on the bench in a house-league sport doesn't come away with a very good feeling.

Sports in many ways represent training for life with choices, rules, successes and failures. Individual and team sports provide much needed exercise with elements of socialization, fun, challenge and sportsmanship. There are as many reasons to play a sport as there are kids.

Some play because they are genuinely interested in the sport, some because of peer pressure and some for parental approval. All parents want to see their

children be successful but shouldn't set the "expectation bar" too high. Children should play for the joy of the game and most of all, the fun. They shouldn't be playing under pressure to realize the lost hopes and glory of their parents.

We have all seen parents at the rink, ball park or soccer field chastising their child for what they perceive to be sub-par play. Sometimes a parent or coach has to identify mistakes for the good of the child's knowledge, understanding of the sport and future performance. Most coaches are well trained and try to be fair, but some get wrapped up in the excitement of the game. Believe it or not, if you are fair and provide an equal playing field, kids will learn a valuable life lesson in being able to evaluate their own abilities.

Let your children try several sports and find out what they are or aren't good at. Allow them to experience playing many different sports and avoid specialization at a young age.

Whatever sport your children choose, focus on helping them to grow as athletes and as people.

CHAPTER NINE

Nutrition & Hydration

Helpful Hydration Hints

Questions are often asked about what to drink, how much and how often during sports, workouts or any physical activity, especially in hot weather. Water is the best, but sports drinks are fine and are certainly much better than sodas.

Approximately 60% of our body weight is water. The recommended average daily intake of water is 8-10 glasses. However, that is just for daily activity and is also necessary throughout the entire year including the winter months.

The summer heat can cause dehydration to sneak up on you at a much faster pace as your body uses up your water supply to keep you cool. Water is to the human body what engine coolant is in your car. It regulates the temperature and prevents over heating.

The first sign of dehydration occurs when you feel thirsty. It can progress quickly with a variety of symptoms like change in complexion, cramps or nausea. If undetected or untreated it can, in extreme cases, result in death. The best advice on suggested water intake for fitness training purposes is in accordance with the guidelines provided by The Canadian Association of Fitness Professionals.

To reduce the risk of dehydration:

- Drink 250-500 ml of water one hour before exercising.
- Drink another 250 ml 20 minutes before exercising.
- Drink 125-250 ml every 15 minutes during the training session.
- Drink one 500 ml bottle of water for every pound lost during the session.

This sounds like a lot of water but the average small bottled water container is 500 ml.

Being properly hydrated assists in respiration, oxygen flow in the blood, endurance, reduces the fatigue level and recuperation time between sessions.

So whether you are participating in team sports, high intensity exercise or just gardening or out for a walk on your lunch hour remember your water bottle and stay hydrated and healthy.

Proper Nutrition + Exercise = Results

We've all heard the saying "You are what you eat". What you eat certainly has an impact when it comes to your workouts. You wouldn't set out on a road trip with your car's gas gauge on empty, so why would you think about working out on an empty stomach?

Whether you workout in the morning, on your lunch breaks or in the evening you need proper nutrition to get the best results. Avoiding eating before or after a workout will not help lose weight. In fact, cutting out meals will create the opposite affect by slowing the body's metabolism to store fat instead of burning it.

To sustain any endurance or aerobic activity, the body first draws on the carbs and then moves to the fat cells for additional energy, popularly referred to as the "fat burning zone". By not eating you have reduced the resource of carbs available and your energy level will quickly be depleted. This causes the blood sugar level to drop, usually accompanied by dizziness or general nausea.

Small snacks an hour before you plan to workout will usually do the trick. A piece of toast with peanut butter, a bran muffin, some fruit, a breakfast bar or bowl of cereal with multi-grain is all you need. During your workout, eating slices of oranges, (common in team sports), is a great way to replenish the fuel supply.

A bottle of water an hour before, one 20 minutes before and a quarter of a bottle for every 15 minutes of your workout will keep the body well hydrated and you're internal cooling system functioning.

The optimal eating pattern would provide for five or six small well-balanced meals per day. With most people's busy schedules this may seem to be unrealistic, but this, like everything else in your day can be accomplished if you plan it out. Many people religiously stick to carefully planned intense fitness regiments only to falter in achieving their best results by not eating either the right foods, portions or at the right time.

If you intend to properly plan your meals allowing for consumption of complex-carbohydrates before your workout, foods such as potatoes, rice, pasta and whole-wheat products are your best choices. They digest easily and provide the fuel your body will need to sustain a 60-minute workout.

Post workout meals should include ample protein products, like chicken or fish to assist in rejuvenation and rebuilding of the muscle tissue.

People with special dietary needs should seek professional advice form their doctors or be referred to registered nutritionists for a diet that is specific to their needs.

Your Calorie Counting Calculation

Most failed attempts to lose weight are as a result of dieting alone. Healthy weight loss for long-term success requires a complete change in lifestyle. Proper diet and nutrition must be accompanied by regular physical activity.

Start by setting realistic goals, both short-term and long-term. If you have a special occasion coming up in the next couple of weeks like a wedding, especially if it's your wedding, and want to lose 20 pounds . . . you've left it too late. Rapid weight loss is extremely stressful on your body and can lead to other health related problems.

A sensible target is to aim for losing one to two pounds of fat a week. One pound of fat equals approximately 3500 calories. If you safely set yourself on a program whereby reducing your daily "net" calories by 500 you will lose a pound of fat a week. "Net" calories refer to the combination of reduced food consumption and calories burnt off by exercising. As an example, if you participated in a fitness program three times a week that burned off 500 calories and reduced your daily calories consumed by 300 you will have accomplished your 3500-calorie (1 pound) weekly reduction. This way you have safely reduced calories and increased your fitness level. Keep in mind that lean muscle gained through exercise speeds up your metabolism and has the additional benefit of burning off more calories even at rest.

The average person should consume between 1500 and 1800 calories each day to properly fuel the body. This is best done with five small meals spread out between breakfast and dinnertime.

Here is a simple formula to estimate the calories you are consuming to maintain your current weight without dieting or factoring in calories expended in a structured fitness program. From this target number you can set some goals as to increasing calories used in exercise and reducing calories by dieting.

Determine your resting metabolic rate (RMR) by multiplying your body weight in pounds by 10 calories.

Example: *A 135 pound moderately active female*

135 lbs X 10 Calories = 1350 Calories used by her daily resting metabolic rate

Now factor in your activity level by adding 20-40% if you are sedentary, 40-60% if you are moderately active and add 60-80% if you are very active.

1350 Calories X 50%) = 675 Calories (Mid-Moderately Active)

Then add the two amounts together.

1350 + 675 = 2025 Calories

With this target number you can now factor in exercise and dieting for a safe weight loss program.

You should always check with your family physician before starting any diet or exercise program, especially if you have special health concerns.

CHAPTER TEN

Helpful Fitness Tips

Sleeping Your Way to Health and Fitness

All too often the forgotten aspect of enhancing your fitness level and incorporating a healthy lifestyle is getting enough rest and sleep.

With today's active lifestyle, work related stress and family commitments our sleep usually takes a back seat. Inadequate sleep leads to lethargy, slower reaction time and decreased energy. Chronic sleep deprivation can lower your body's immune system leaving you susceptible to diseases and illness. If you are not getting the sleep you need, try some of these tips:

- Don't nap during the day, as it will produce fragmented sleep. Try to keep all of your sleep for bedtime to allow for continuity in your sleep pattern.

- Eliminate or reduce the consumption of caffeine (tea, coffee, soft drinks, etc.) after lunch as it acts as a stimulant not a relaxant.

- Avoid snacking late at night as it keeps the digestive system alert and can interfere with your sleep pattern.

- Don't do excessive or high intensity exercise within four hours of bedtime as it revs up the metabolism making it difficult to fall asleep.

- Avoid working on your computer before bedtime or having your computer in the bedroom. The computer's light stimulates the brain and having it in the bedroom creates a link with work and not rest.

- Try to keep regular sleep patterns by going to bed and waking at the same time each day. Your body craves regularity, sleeping in on the weekend throws off your body's circadian rhythm, which in turn causes changes to your eating habits.

- Keep the bedroom temperature cool. Many people believe keeping the bedroom warm helps them fall asleep. Studies show that you will get a deeper uninterrupted sleep if you keep the temperature cooler than the rest of your home.

- Disconnect the snooze button on your clock radio and get up when the alarm goes off. Hitting 'snooze' disrupts rest, and you'd be better served by staying in a deep sleep.

Most of all try to get eight hours sleep each night. Allow your body to get the much-needed rest it requires to get you through your next busy day.

Injuries - Prevention and Treatment

Ironically, staying active for fitness and health benefits sometimes results in injuries. No matter how fit you are or how careful, it is inevitable that you will occasionally sustain an injury.

There are basically two types of injuries: acute and chronic. An acute injury occurs suddenly during a specific movement and you know you have strained a muscle, ligament or tendon. The pain can range from mild to intense. If the pain is severe stop immediately and consult a physician. If it is mild you may wish to treat it using the R.I.C.E. method.

Rest begins the healing process and limits further damage.

Ice will reduce swelling. Icing the area is effective for the first 72 hours. Ice the area for 10-20 minutes several times during the day.

Compression will also help reduce swelling by applying pressure by hand or using a tensor bandage.

Elevation will prevent the pooling of blood around the injured area.

Chronic injuries are usually attributed to overuse and repetitive use. These types of injuries most commonly occur in the joints or in the lower back. Lower back injuries can be acute but generally are sustained as a result of poor posture and insufficient or improper exercise. Chronic injuries can seem very insignificant at first but as they linger the discomfort will increase and left untreated can advance to have disabling effects. If you have had a specific injury that just won't seem to go away or just gets better and is re-injured you should see your physician.

Practising the following tips can significantly reduce injuries:

- Choose a program that is right for your fitness level. Starting at a lower level than you feel capable of will be more beneficial than to jumping in over your head and risking injury that will delay your progress.

- Select a program that is specifically designed for you. Change your routine every 8-12 weeks.

- Learn proper technique, form and exercise selection.

- Evaluate the equipment you are using. Is it safe? Are the cables, worn or frayed? Are all the weight plates and collars secure?

- Ensure your exercise room is well ventilated and properly lighted. Eliminate distraction and keep the area free of objects to trip over or strike during movements.

- Warm-up properly for 7-10 minutes to allow your body to prepare for the workout by increasing the body temperature, warming the muscles and elevating the heart rate.

- Stretch thoroughly after the workout to allow your body to cool down and restore the natural length to the muscle groups used.

Frequently Asked Questions - Fitness Clubs vs Home Gyms

Should I workout at a gym or at home?

There is no right answer. If you do not want to be disturbed perhaps the home gym is ideal for you. On the other hand some people require a group setting to get motivated.

Obviously, the equipment selection at the gym is going to be far superior to most home gyms. The question then is do you need all the specialized equipment or does the equipment at home meet your needs? Gyms offer variety and professional supervision, as most clubs now offer personal training or a program design setup. Home gyms usually come with a workout booklet. Videos, fitness books, Internet programs or even a personal training session can start you off on the right program.

The bottom line is, you can train at a gym or at home and get the results you want by putting in the time to research your needs and selecting the option that best suits those needs.

What equipment do I need to work out at home?

There are numerous home gyms on the market. Go to fitness stores, try them out and get the staff to show you how they work. Don't get caught up in buying every piece of equipment advertised on TV.

The standard multi-station home gym is more than sufficient. If space is a concern you can opt for free weights, a stability ball, resistance tubing and a step. To work on your cardio you can buy a stationary bike, treadmill, walk, jog or bike.

Most importantly, buy something you will use. If cost is a concern, check out garage sales. You don't need to take out a mortgage to equip your gym.

What should I be looking for in a fitness club?

When deciding on a gym or fitness club consider the four A's: Accessibility, Availability, Attractiveness and Affordability.

Accessibility:

Is it easy and convenient to get to? Can you walk or bike there, or do you need to drive?

Availability:

Is it open at lunch hour or early morning when you want to workout? Does it have the equipment you need?

Attractiveness:

Is it clean, well maintained and safe?

Affordability:

Is it in your price range? Do they offer monthly, 3, 6 or 12 month memberships, or student and/or seniors discounts?

Choosing a Personal Trainer

Personal trainers are no longer exclusive to the wealthy. Many people in normal walks of life utilize the services of a personal trainer. Some just want a trainer to design a personalized training program, provide equipment instruction, demonstrate safe and proper techniques or design a sport specific program. Others may be looking for weight loss and fat reduction, improved health or motivation and commitment to start an exercise program.

To choose a personal trainer you can check the phone directory, Internet or ask around at gyms and fitness centres. Be careful not to have someone that is uncertified act as your trainer.

Ask to see their certification card. The Canadian Association of Fitness Professionals (CanFitPro), Canadian Personal Trainers Network (CPTN) and The American Council on Exercise (ACE), are all recognized certifications.

Choosing a certified personal trainer provides you with someone who has received education in program design and instruction in resistance training, cardiovascular training and flexibility as well as physical anatomy and nutrition. They have also demonstrated competence in written theory and practical application to a high standard. Positive results will be increased and incidence of injury decreased.

For a personal trainer to maintain their certification requires constant upgrading with a minimum of four Continuing Education Credits per year. This involves attending courses, workshops, seminars and trade shows to keeps current on new

trends, techniques, equipment, research and resources, which are all passed on to you the client.

Ask for experience and references, fitness clubs they have worked at and programs they have developed. Do they have specialization in specific sports; have they worked with older adults, groups or individuals?

Ask if they are insured through an association or independent. They must provide proof of certification to be insured.

Male and female trainers are equally qualified so choose one you are comfortable working with.

Lastly, insist on a contract outlining fees, payment schedules, duration of sessions and cancellation policy. A contract protects both you and the trainer from a misrepresentation and/or a simple misunderstanding.

Winter Cold Weather Exercise Tips

With the cold of winter comes shorter daylight hours. If you work inside during the day make sure you get outside on your breaks and lunch for some sunlight, fresh winter air and maybe even a brisk little walk.

For those of you who religiously get to the gym, keep up the good work and try to entice a friend to go with you.

If you are the type that loves the outdoors, there is no reason to let the cold weather stop you from getting out and enjoying your favorite winter activity.

Before heading out to brave the winter elements consider these three things: Clothing, Temperature and Hydration.

1. Clothing:

When preparing to go out to the slopes, trails or just to an outdoor skating rink consider your selection of clothing. Material such as cotton and silk tend to hold moisture close to the skin and will contribute to lowering your body temperature. Wool, polypropylene and polyester tend to keep sweat away from the body maintaining the core temperature. Most heat loss comes from the head so be sure to wear a warm hat. The face, hands and feet are the most susceptible to frostbite so make sure you have a scarf, mittens or gloves and a warm pair of insulated boots.

2. Temperature :

Don't be fooled just because it's sunny out there, be sure to take into account the wind-chill factor. Frostbite or hypothermia can set in rapidly when your body temperature drops below 95 degrees Fahrenheit. Be cautious and watch for signs of hypothermia which can include difficulty in speaking, slowed heart rate and breathing, loss of coordination and a disoriented mental state.

3. Hydration :

A common misconception is that you can't become dehydrated when it is cold . . . Wrong! It is just as important to stay hydrated in cold weather as it is in warm weather. Just because you can't see the sweat in cold weather, your body is still losing fluid during physical activity. Stick to consuming water in the same quantity that you would throughout the year. The old idea of drinking alcohol to warm you up is completely wrong. Although you may feel like the alcohol is warming you up, it actually does the opposite. Alcohol actually causes the blood vessels in your extremities and skin to open up causing drastic heat loss. See "Helpful Hydration Hints" on page 35.

Summer Hot Weather Exercise Tips

When working out or participating in sports during the summer months one should consider several factors. _Hydration_ is the most important issue and requires the constant consumption of fluids. Sports drinks are fine they but take longer to be absorbed into your system, while soft drinks will only make you thirstier. As boring as it may seem, the best drink to consume is water. See "Helpful Hydration Hints" on page 35.

Incidents of dehydration can be reduced if you drink 250-500 ml of water one hour before exercising. Drink another 250 ml 20 minutes before and 125-250 ml every 15 minutes during the training session. If you are an outdoor fitness enthusiast or workout at home without the benefit of air-conditioning, take caution when it comes to the time of your workout.

Reduce the overall time spent on the program and try to do your routine in the morning or evening when the temperatures are a little lower.

Clothing is another consideration as some people are under a misconception they have to really sweat to get a good workout and will wear track pants and a sweatshirt, even in the summer. . .Wrong. Dress light and concentrate on just getting a good workout.

You can also consider water sports as a cool alternative to a traditional workout, still getting a good cardio or resistance workout and keeping your body temperature down at the same time.

Whatever activity you choose, stay hydrated, wear sunscreen, a hat, stay cool and stay healthy.

Fitness Motivation Tips

Most people starting out on a new fitness plan will reach a pivotal time 6-8 weeks into their program. Ask yourself the following questions to assess your program and motivate you to continue:

- Have I accentuated the positive and let go of the negative? Thinking and believing you can do it will carry over into positive results.

- Have I set short-term and long-term goals and rewards? What do I want to do: lose weight, gain muscle, tone or participate in a sport? Now set rewards like buying new clothes or dining out.

- Have I focused on attainable and realistic goals so that way my rewards won't be too elusive? Motivation will be derived from gaining those little rewards you set for yourself along the way. See "Fitting SMART Fitness Goals into Your Program" on page 8.

- Have I tailored a workout that lets me achieve my goals and rewards? Choose an activity or sport you enjoy, as you will be more likely to stick to it. Weight training for muscle gain, cardio for weight loss. If you want to lose weight and tone, you should combine both (cross-training).

- Have I tried something new to keep my program fresh or should I find a workout partner with similar goals and interests to inject commitment into my routine?

- Have I chosen the right workout environment? If you like solitude, you may want to purchase some workout equipment, a home gym or fitness videos to exercise in the privacy of your home. If you like the social aspect you may want a gym membership that offers a variety of equipment and classes.

- Have I scheduled my workouts and consider them to be an important part of my day? Your health, self-image and stress reduction should be important to you.

Now that you have assessed your program you should get yourself mentally prepared. Instead of thinking of it as: "I've got to do it", psyche yourself up that you want to do it and remember how good you feel after the workout.

Record a journal to keep you accountable and push you to stay on track. You should keep track of your entire food and caloric intake as well as your (F.I.T.T.) exercise Frequency, Intensity, Time and Type. Your journal is also a great indicator of what is working and what isn't. See "Keeping a Fitness Journal" on page 10.

"Two of a Kind" Partner Training

Working out can sometimes feels like a chore. For many people it's tough to put aside the daily grind and take time for fitness. Let's look at the issue of time. There are 168 hours in each week. If you could manage to squeeze in just 30 minutes a day of some form of physical activity, that would leave you with 164 ½ hours a week to get everything else done. When you look at it that way it doesn't seem so time consuming, does it?

We've all heard the phrase: "Two heads are better than one". Well, sometimes it

takes two to get motivated and get fit. First, choose a training partner with similar goals and fitness interests. If you want to be a body builder and your partner is training to run a marathon. . .well you get the point.

Before starting out on your new program set and share your goals with your partner. This way you and your partner become more accountable for each other's success. Training with friends or your spouse can provide for excellent quality time together while working towards a common goal. Your commitment level will also likely increase when you know you have someone expecting you to be ready to workout. While you are working out with a partner there is also the tendency to work a little harder and push each other to lift a few more pounds or run at a little quicker pace.

Each person has different areas of knowledge or experience to offer to the other. You may both read different publications or have subscriptions to health and fitness magazines that you can share. There are even some gyms, clubs or trainers that will offer two for one memberships and programs encouraging couples participation that make teaming up an affordable option.

The safety aspect of your workout increases as well. Accidents do happen, so the buddy system can be a lifesaver. If your goals include resistance training, remember, when lifting heavy weights a spotter is always a wise idea. Even if you aren't into weights, a partner can be there in case of an emergency, like heart problems or a fall. There is also safety in numbers if you are walking or running outside at night.

Fit-Break for the Home Based Business

Currently, the home based business sector is experiencing tremendous growth. But starting your own business is very stressful and short exercise breaks can help relieve stress. Long periods in your home office, on the phone or using the computer are fatiguing. Exercise will re-energize you and release endorphins to help prevent mood swings or depression and help you focus.

Often, in a one person or family business you don't have the luxury of health benefits or paid sick days. Staying healthy and avoiding being run down is crucial to success. Make fit-breaks your business.

This 10-minute exercise program, one minute for each exercise, can be done in your office and works all the muscles. It can be performed 1-3 times a day for a great fit-break instead of a coffee break.

All you need is your chair and your body. Try to do 10-15 repetitions of each exercise with slow movement, remembering to exhale on exertion.

1. *Side Leg Raises* :
Stand, bring one leg out to side and back to standing position, repeat.

2. *Leg Crossovers* :
Stand, bring one leg over in front of the other leg and back to standing position, repeat.

3. *Front Extensions* :
Bring knee up parallel to floor, extend leg out straight, back to standing position, repeat.

4. *Rear Extensions* :
Stand, keep back straight, raise leg to rear and back, repeat.

5. *Chair Squats* :
Stand with hands on chair, bend knees to squat position using chair for support and back up, repeat.

6. *Chair Lunges* :
Stand with hands on chair, bend knees to side lunge position using chair for support and back up, alternate sides.

7. *Wall Pushups* :
Place hands against wall, arms length away and lean forward, bring nose close to wall and push off, repeat.

8. *Standing Arm Circles Front* :
Large circles, alternate direction.

9. *Arm Raises* :
Side, overhead, front and back.

10. Side Bends :

One hand down side, other hand raised up and behind head, bend to side, repeat, then other side.

Also, remember to drink more water and less coffee. Staying hydrated helps your concentration and alertness.

Taking Vacation Time for Yourself

The first and most important thing is to actually take a vacation. All work and no play leads to "Burn Out" which can be counter-productive. This is an all too common problem these days. Although we may believe the world will stop if we aren't available for work each day, surprisingly it will roll along just fine without us.

Vacation is a time to allow your body and mind a chance to relax and rejuvenate. "Burn Out" is not exclusive to the "Workaholic". Most people usually take time off in one-week periods to spread it out so as to not seem like it's over in one shot and have to wait another year for their next vacation. Others break it up because taking more than a week at a time is just not convenient for their employers. Studies have concluded that your body needs two full weeks away from the daily stressors, cell phones, pagers, laptops, etc. to become properly rested.

If you have convinced yourself that a vacation is necessary, then what about your workouts? Most people who are fitness conscious and committed to an exercise program will find something to keep them active. The old saying: "A change is as good as a rest" comes in handy here. Just about any place you choose to vacation will provide new and different opportunities for physical activity.

Hotels usually have fitness centres with weights, cardio machines and some even provide aerobics classes allowing you to try new equipment in a new environment that will hit the muscles slightly differently than what you are used to.

If cottaging is your choice, water sports such as swimming or water skiing, beach activities like volleyball, touch football or Frisbee can be fun and effective workouts combining strength, cardio and flexibility.

Some prefer to stay home and do day trips or get the stuff done around the house that there never seems to be time for. If you are day tripping, like going to an amusement park, the zoo or trail hiking you will put a lot of kilometres on your feet and your heart will thank you. So do yourself a favour and take some time off, you'll come back healthier and more productive.

Don't let your fitness level get away from you by taking the summer off completely, with no activity. It is a lot easier to stay in shape than it is to get in shape. If you've been working out 3-5 times a week during the winter, you can easily cut down the workouts to 2-3 without losing much of what you've gained.

You can also change your routine by continuing to work out as often but reduce the time spent and number of sets. Alternatively you could cut the workouts down but increase the intensity.

Either way you are maintaining your gains. If you're playing slow pitch, golfing, walking, running, swimming or bicycling outside in the beautiful summer weather you are also contributing to maintaining your fitness level.

Remember that your fitness and health will diminish when you either cut out the regular exercise all together or over-train and fail to give your body the rest and recovery time it needs.

CHAPTER ELEVEN

Equipment & Hand Wrapping

Guidelines for Equipment Selection

Ensure all Equipment is in Good Condition and Fits Properly

Round-Timer :

Select a round-timer that can be set for two or three minute rounds with 30 or 60 second rests and has lights: green for the start of the round; yellow for the 30 seconds remaining warning; and red for the end of the round.

There are also CD's on the market that are programmed with music that starts and ends to signal rounds and rests.

Skipping Ropes :

Skipping ropes come in either plastic or leather. Choose the length according to your height: 8 foot ropes for people 5' 4" and under; 9 foot ropes for 5' 5" to 6 feet; and a 10 foot rope if you are over 6 feet tall.

If in doubt, buy the longer rope as you can always wrap it around your hand to shorten it.

Gloves :

8 to 20 ounce gloves with Velcro or lace are available, but 10 or 12 ounce boxing gloves, preferably with Velcro wrists for quick change, are best.

Hand Wraps :

Hand wraps provide support for the wrist and small bones in the hands. They range from 108" to 180" in length. Always choose a longer length, as more wrap is more protection.

Forearm Shields or Focus Pads :

Shields and pads provide a target for the striker and absorb the impact of the punches and strikes. They come in various sizes and thickness. Be sure the thickness matches the force that will be applied to avoid injury to the holder.

Focus pads are usually sold by ounces: 12, 14 and 16 ounce sizes. Forearm shields are usually 16"-18" long, 10"-12" in width and 2"-3" thick. Velcro straps are best for quick adjustments and changes. Use kicking shields for heavy kicking drills.

Footwear :

You can wear cross trainers with light tread or regulation boxing or kickboxing shoes. Bare feet are acceptable but kick-boots will help prevent injury.

Equipment & Hand Wrapping

Attire :

You can wear loose fitting pants or shorts, and a t-shirt. Or, if you prefer, boxing and kickboxing apparel are also available.

Music :

Aerobic boxing/kickboxing music with a 132-144 beats per minute even 32 count can be used during your workout. Or you can simply use whatever type of music motivates you.

Free-Standing Portable Heavy Bags :

Free-standing bags come in various shapes and sizes ranging from cylindrical, cone shaped and even with replica upper body form that you can fill with water or sand to the desired weight.

Whichever type you choose, make sure it is adjustable in height.

Hanging Heavy Bags :

Hanging bags range in sizes from 50 pounds up to approximately 150 pounds. They are made of leather or canvass and can also come in water filled style. A mid range 80-100 pound leather bag is best for wear.

Medicine Balls :

Medicine balls range from 1 to 30 pounds and can be made of leather which do not bounce or of rubber which provide some bounce. The 4-6 pound rubber balls are the best all purpose balls that will suit most people's needs.

Stability Balls :

Choose an anti-burst stability ball that will hold at least two to three times your body weight. As a guideline for sizing: if you are under 5'4" choose a 55 cm ball; 5'5" to 5'11" choose a 65 cm ball; and if you are over 6' go with a 75 cm ball.

Make sure it is fully inflated and when you are seated on the ball your thighs are parallel to the floor. If in doubt choose a ball that ensures that when you are seated your hips are slightly above your knees.

Resistance Tubing :

Resistance tubing Is available in five different levels of resistance from very light to very heavy. Medium resistance is most common and tubing with handles is best for the exercises described in this book.

Agility Ladders :

These ladders come in 15 foot lengths and are made of either canvass or cloth with wood or plastic adjustable rungs.

Mini-Hurdles :

Mini-hurdles are usually plastic, 6" high with available attachments for an additional 6" in height. Keeping the height to 6" keeps the pace quick and reduces the impact when you land.

Weave Poles :

Weave poles are made of plastic or wood, are 6' feet in length, and can be quickly inserted into their bases. The poles help keep you in an upright position as opposed to pylons which people have a tendency to hunch over when navigating around.

Hand Wrapping

Left Hand   **Right Hand**

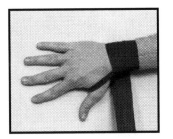

1. Start with loop over thumb and wrap across the back of the hand with 3 wraps around the wrist.

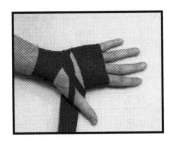

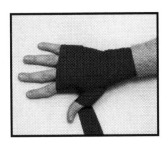

2. Wrap around the knuckles 3 times.

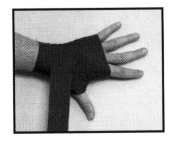

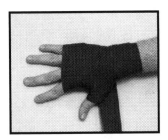

3. Wrap back around wrist in to top of thumb and back and figure 8 across hand.

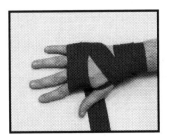

4 Wrap back over thumb and back and figure 8 across hand.

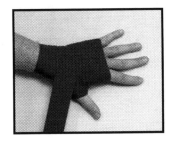

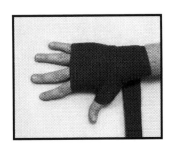

5 Continue to wrap in figure 8 motion and complete with 3 wraps around wrist securing with Velcro.

CHAPTER TWELVE

Punching & Kicking Techniques

Fighting Stance

1. Feet are shoulder width apart in a balanced position, knees slightly bent.

2. Lead foot forward shoulder width ahead of back foot bladed slightly to the 1:00 o'clock position.

NOTES : Photographs shown are depicting a left foot forward stance most common to a right handed fighter. The position can be reversed for a left handed fighter. For best fitness results the fighter should use both stances equally during the class or session.

Foot position is at 11:00 o'clock for left handed fighters.

The Jab

1. Start in fighting stance. Hands in guard position.

2. Extend the lead arm straight out rotating the hand palm down. Keep the rear hand up in the guard position.

3. Retract the arm and return to the fighting stance. Hands in guard position.

The Cross

1. Start in fighting stance. Hands in guard position.

2. Extend the rear arm straight forward with the hand palm down. Rotate the rear hip forward while pivoting on the balls of the feet.

3. Retract the arm and return to the fighting stance. Hands in guard position.

NOTE: Photographs shown are depicting a left foot forward stance most common to a right handed fighter. The position can be reversed for a left handed fighter. For best fitness results the fighter should use both stances equally during the class or session.

The Hook

1. Start in fighting stance. Hands in guard position.

2. Drop the shoulder and raise forearm palm down. Start to pivot on the balls of the feet.

3. Pivot the lead hip forward keeping the arm parallel to the floor and the arm in an 80–100 degree position.

4. Retract the arm and return to fighting stance. Hands in guard position.

NOTES : The hook can be executed with either the lead hand or rear hand.

Photographs shown are depicting a lead hand left hook with the left foot forward stance most common to a right handed fighter. The position can be reversed for a left handed fighter. For best fitness results the fighter should use both stances equally during the class or session.

The Uppercut

1. Start in fighting stance. Hands in guard position.

2. Drop the shoulder and the forearm by crouching slightly. Start to pivot on the balls of the feet.

3. Pivot the rear hip forward keeping the arm flexed. Push with the hips and as you drive the hand upward rotate the hand position completing the punch with the palm facing you.

4. Retract the arm and return to fighting stance. Hands in guard position.

NOTES : The uppercut can be executed with either the lead hand or rear hand.

Photographs shown are depicting a rear hand uppercut with the left foot forward stance most common to a right handed fighter. The position can be reversed for a left handed fighter. For best fitness results the fighter should use both stances equally during the class or session.

The Lead Leg Front Snap Kick

1. Start in fighting stance. Hands in guard position.

2. Raise the front knee pointing it at the intended target. Shift the bodyweight to the rear leg and point the toes downward.

3. Extend the leg and strike the target with the instep. (On the shoe laces)

4. Retract the kicking leg.

5. Return to fighting stance. Hands in guard position.

NOTES : The front snap kick can be executed with either the lead leg or rear leg.

Photographs shown are depicting a lead leg snap kick with the left foot forward stance most common to a right handed fighter. The position can be reversed for a left handed fighter. For best fitness results the fighter should use both stances equally during the class or session.

The lead leg snap kick should be performed until proficient before implementing the more powerful rear leg snap kick.

The Roundhouse Kick (Lead Leg)

1. Start in fighting stance. Hands in guard position.

2. Raise the front knee pointing it at the intended target. Begin to pivot the base foot away from the target.

3. Extend the leg and strike the target with the instep, while completing the pivot. (Strike on the shoe laces)

4. Retract the kicking leg.

5. Return to fighting stance. Hands in guard position.

NOTES : The round kick is executed with the lead leg; the roundhouse is executed with the rear leg.

Photographs shown are depicting a lead leg round kick with the left foot forward stance most common to a right handed fighter. The position can be reversed for a left handed fighter. For best fitness results the fighter should use both stances equally during the class or session.

The lead leg round kick should be performed until proficient before implementing the more powerful rear leg roundhouse kick.

The Rear Leg Front Snap Kick

1. Start in fighting stance. Hands in guard position.

2. Raise the rear knee pointing it at the intended target. Shift the body weight to the front leg and point the toes downward.

3. Extend the leg and strike the target with the instep. (On the shoe laces)

4. Retract the kicking leg.

5. Return to fighting stance. Hands in guard position.

NOTES: The front snap kick can be executed with either the lead leg or rear leg.

Photographs shown are depicting a rear leg snap kick with the left foot forward stance most common to a right handed fighter. The position can be reversed for a left handed fighter. For best fitness results the fighter should use both stances equally during the class or session.

The lead leg snap kick should be performed until proficient before implementing the more powerful rear leg snap kick.

The Knee Strike

1. Start in fighting stance. Hands in guard position.

2. Drop the hands to grab the target, crouching slightly.

3. Pivot the rear hip forward bending the knee. Push with the hips as you drive the knee upward and pull the target downward. Lean back slightly as you strike for more power.

4. Retract the knee and return to fighting stance. Hands in guard position.

NOTES: The knee strike can be executed with either knee, but the most power is generated from the rear knee.

Photographs shown are depicting a rear knee strike with the left foot forward stance most common to a right handed fighter. The position can be reversed for a left handed fighter. For best fitness results the fighter should use both stances equally during the class or session.

CHAPTER THIRTEEN

Pad Holding & Heavy Bags

Kicks: Pad Holding & Foot Placement

Round/Roundhouse Kick:
Pad held to kicker's height with the
arm flexed 45 to 90 degrees and
away from the body. (Foot placement
should match the kicker - place
the same foot forward)

Snap Kick and Knee Strike:
Pads held stacked on top of each
other with the lead hand on the
bottom and the rear hand supporting
supporting on top. (Foot placement
should match the kicker/striker - place
the same foot forward)

NOTE: Photographs shown are depicting a left foot forward stance most common to a right
handed fighter.

Kicks: Fighter & Pad Holder Positions

Fighting Stance & Pad Holder Stance: With Same Foot Forward

Lead Leg Front Snap

NOTE: Photographs shown are depicting a left foot forward stance most common to a right handed fighter. The position can be reversed for a left handed fighter. For best fitness results the fighter should use both stances equally during the class or session.

Kicks: Fighter & Pad Holder Positions (Continued)

Rear Leg Front Kick

Lead Leg Round Kick

NOTE: Photographs shown are depicting a left foot forward stance most common to a right handed fighter. The position can be reversed for a left handed fighter. For best fitness results the fighter should use both stances equally during the class or session.

Kicks: **Fighter & Pad Holder Positions** (Continued)

Rear Leg Roundhouse Kick

Rear Leg Knee Strike

NOTE: Photographs shown are depicting a left foot forward stance most common to a right handed fighter. The position can be reversed for a left handed fighter. For best fitness results the fighter should use both stances equally during the class or session.

Evasive Techniques: Fighter & Pad Holder Positions

Step Out Evasive Technique

Slip a Left Jab

NOTE: Photographs shown are depicting a left foot forward stance most common to a right handed fighter. The position can be reversed for a left handed fighter. For best fitness results the fighter should use both stances equally during the class or session.

Evasive Techniques: Fighter & Pad Holder Positions
(Continued)

Slip a Right Cross

Duck a Hook

NOTE: Photographs shown are depicting a left foot forward stance most common to a right handed fighter. The position can be reversed for a left handed fighter. For best fitness results the fighter should use both stances equally during the class or session.

Punches: Pad Holding & Foot Placement

Jab: Pad held head high angled to the shoulder of the puncher with feet in a position matching the puncher. (Lead hand)

Cross: Pad held head high angled to the shoulder of the puncher with feet in a position matching the puncher. (Rear hand)

Hook: Pad held chin high with the arm flexed to 90 degrees in tight to the body. (Can be performed with either the lead or rear hand)

Uppercut: Pad held on rear hand chin high palm down. (Can be performed with either the lead or rear hand)

NOTE: Foot position should always match that of the puncher - same foot forward.

Punches: Boxer & Pad Holder Positions

Jab

Cross

NOTE: Photographs shown are depicting a left foot forward stance most common to a right handed fighter. The position can be reversed for a left handed fighter. For best fitness results the fighter should use both stances equally during the class or session.

Punches: Boxer & Pad Holder Positions (Continued)

Hook

Uppercut

NOTE: Photographs shown are depicting a left foot forward stance most common to a right handed fighter. The position can be reversed for a left handed fighter. For best fitness results the fighter should use both stances equally during the class or session.

Heavy Bag Punches

Jab

Cross

Hook

Uppercut

CHAPTER FOURTEEN

Boxing Combinations

Boxing Combination - # 1
Jab, Cross (1 - 2)

Fighting Stance

Jab

Cross

Fighting Stance

Boxing Combination - # 2

Jab, Cross, Hook (1 - 2 - 3)

Fighting Stance

Jab

Cross

Hook

Fighting Stance

Boxing Combination - # 3
Jab, Cross, Hook, Uppercut (1 - 2 - 3 - 4)

Fighting Stance

Jab

Cross

Hook

Uppercut

Fighting Stance

Boxing Combination - # 4
Jab, Out, Jab, Cross (1 - Out - 1 - 2)

Fighting Stance

Jab

Step Out Evasive Technique

Jab

Cross

Fighting Stance

Boxing Combination - # 5
Jab, Cross, Slip, Slip, Jab, Cross (1 - 2 - Slip - Slip - 1 - 2)

Jab

Cross

Slip a Left Jab

Slip a Right Cross

Jab

Cross

NOTE : Start and finish the combination with the Fighting Stance.

Boxing Combination - # 6
Jab, Cross, Duck, Cross (1 - 2 - Over - 2)

Fighting Stance

Jab

Cross

Duck a Hook

Cross

Fighting Stance

Boxing Combination - # 7
Jab, Slip, Jab, Cross (1 - Slip - 1 - 2)

Fighting Stance

Jab

Slip a Right Cross

Jab

Cross

Fighting Stance

Boxing Combination - # 8

Jab, Cross, Slip, Cross (1 - 2 - Slip - 2)

Fighting Stance

Jab

Cross

Slip a Left Jab

Cross

Fighting Stance

CHAPTER FIFTEEN

Kickboxing Combinations

Kickboxing Combination - # 1
Front Snap - Cross

Fighting Stance

Lead Leg Front Snap

Cross

Fighting Stance

Kickboxing Combination - # 2

Front Snap - Jab - Cross

Fighting Stance

Lead Leg Front Snap

Jab

Cross

Fighting Stance

Kickboxing Combination - # 3
Front Snap - Jab - Cross - Hook - Rear Roundhouse

Fighting Stance

Lead Leg Front Snap

Jab

Cross

Hook

Rear Leg Roundhouse Kick

NOTE: Finish the combination with the Fighting Stance.

Kickboxing Combination - # 4
Front Snap - Jab - Uppercut - Rear Knee Strike

Fighting Stance

Lead Leg Front Snap

Jab

Uppercut

Rear Leg Knee Strike

Fighting Stance

Kickboxing Combination - # 5
Front Snap - Lead Round - Jab - Cross

Fighting Stance

Lead Leg Front Snap

Lead Leg Round Kick

Jab

Cross

Fighting Stance

Kickboxing Combination - # 6
Jab - Front Snap - Rear Snap - Rear Knee

Fighting Stance

Jab

Lead Leg Front Snap

Rear Leg Front Kick

Rear Leg Knee Strike

Fighting Stance

Kickboxing Combination - # 7
Jab - Cross - Front Snap - Rear Roundhouse

Fighting Stance

Jab

Cross

Lead Leg Front Snap

Rear Leg Roundhouse Kick

Fighting Stance

Kickboxing Combination - # 8
Jab - Cross - Hook - Rear Knee

Fighting Stance

Jab

Cross

Hook

Rear Leg knee Strike

Fighting Stance

CHAPTER SIXTEEN

Agility Exercises

Agility Ladder – In-In-Out-Out

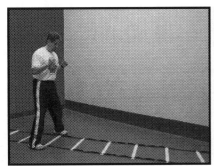

Both feet outside ladder.

Right foot in.

Left foot in.

Right foot out and forward to the next square on the ladder.

Left foot out and forward to the next square on the ladder.

NOTE: Can be performed in sets or timed 30, 45 or 60 second circuits.

Agility Ladder – Hop Scotch

Both feet out.   Both feet in.   Move forward to the next square with both feet out.

NOTE: Can be performed in sets or timed 30, 45 or 60 second circuits.

Agility Ladder – Side Step Shuffle

Continuously move either left or right down the squares in the agility ladder, never landing both feet in the same square.

NOTE: Can be performed in sets or timed 30, 45 or 60 second circuits.

Agility Weave Poles

Maintaining a proper fighting guard, navigate through the weave poles.

NOTE: Can be performed in sets or timed 30, 45 or 60 second circuits.

Mini-Hurdles

Mini-hurdles are positioned so that the athlete can run placing one foot down between jumps.

NOTE: Can be performed in sets or timed 30, 45 or 60 second circuits.

CHAPTER SEVENTEEN

Resistance Training Exercises

Stability Ball – Seated Leg Extension Front Kick

(Quadriceps)

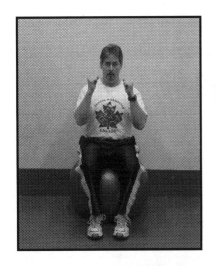

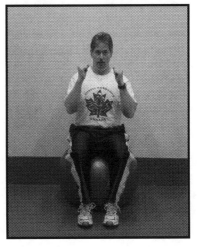

Seated on the stability ball, raise your left knee. Extend your leg, pointing your toe to replicate a front kick. Retract your leg and return to the start position. Switch legs, and repeat.

NOTE: You can add ankle weights or resistance tubing for more intensity.

Stability Ball – Squat

(Quadriceps, Hamstrings & Glutes)

Place the stability ball against the wall, positioned in the small of your back. Walk your feet forward until your body weight is resting against the ball. Position your feet hip width apart. Squat until your thighs are parallel to the floor and press upward. Do not let your knees go past your toes and keep your back straight. Rise up, return to the start position, and repeat.

NOTE: You can add dumbbells or resistance tubing for more intensity.

Stability Ball – Lunge

(Quadriceps, Hamstrings & Glutes)

Place the stability ball against the wall, positioned in the small of your back. Place your right foot back, with your toe on the floor and your heal against the wall. Your left foot is comfortably forward. Lunge, bringing your right knee to the floor, making sure your left knee does not go past your toes. Rise up, return to the start position, and repeat. Switch legs, and repeat.

Stability Ball – Side Kick

(Adductors, Abbductors & Glutes)

Position your body with your right side leaning on the stability ball, and your left knee and right lower leg on the floor. With your hands in the guard position, raise your knee to the retracted position. Extend your leg with full range of motion, ensuring the outside edge of your heel is pointing away. Retract your leg and return to the start position, and repeat. Switch sides, and repeat.

NOTE: You can add ankle weights or resistance tubing for more intensity.

Stability Ball – Roundhouse Kick

(Quadriceps & Glutes)

Position your body with your right side leaning on the stability ball, and your left knee and right lower leg on the floor. With your hands in the guard position, raise your knee to the retracted position with your knee pointed in the direction of the target. Fully extend your leg with your toes pointed. Retract your leg and return to the start position, and repeat. Switch sides, and repeat.

NOTE: You can add ankle weights or resistance tubing for more intensity.

Stability Ball – Squeeze & Punch

(Adductors)

Position your body with your legs straddling the stability ball and your hands in the guard position. Squeeze the stability ball between your thighs while punching, alternating hands.

NOTE: You can add wrist weights or resistance tubing for more intensity.

Resistance Tubing – Side-Step

(Adductors)

Start by placing the resistance tubing securely under your feet and hold one handle in each hand. Maintaining a minimum of hip width apart, step to your left. Bring your left foot back to the start position. Maintaining a minimum of hip width apart, step to your right. Bring your right foot back to the start position, and repeat.

Resistance Tubing – Rear Kick

(Quadriceps, Hamstrings & Glutes)

While on your hands and knees, place the resistance tubing securely under one foot and hold one handle in each hand. Fully extend your left leg to the rear with your toes pointing down, as though striking with your heel. Retract your leg and return to the start position, and repeat. Switch legs, and repeat.

Resistance Tubing – Bench Press

(Pectorals)

Stand with your feet a comfortable distance apart. With the resistance tubing going around your back and under your arms, hold one handle in each hand. Raise your arms parallel to the floor to replicate the body position as though performing a flat bench press lying supine on a bench. Ensure the resistance tubing has sufficient tension by shortening up your grip. Press both hands straight forward and bring your thumbs together at your body's midline. Retract and return to the start position, and repeat.

Resistance Tubing – Flyes

(Pectorals)

Stand with your feet a comfortable distance apart. With the resistance tubing going around your back and under your arms, hold one handle in each hand. Raise your arms parallel to the floor to replicate the body position as though performing a flat bench flye lying supine on a bench. Ensure the resistance tubing has sufficient tension by shortening up your grip. Bring your hands together in an arcing motion until your palms meet at your body's midline. Retract and return to the start position, and repeat.

Resistance Tubing – Seated Lat Row

(Upper Back & Laterals)

 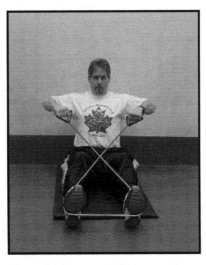 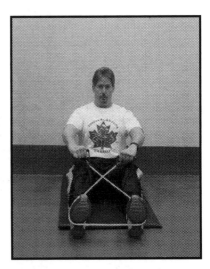

Sit on the floor with your feet hip width apart. Wrap the resistance tubing securely under both feet. Cross the resistance tubing and hold one handle in each hand, with your palms down and arms parallel to the floor. Row back, ensuring full retraction of the shoulder blades. Return to the start position, and repeat.

Resistance Tubing – Seated Two Arm Row

(Mid Back & Rhomboids)

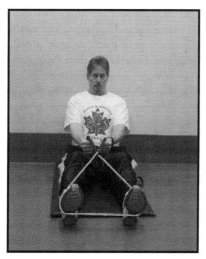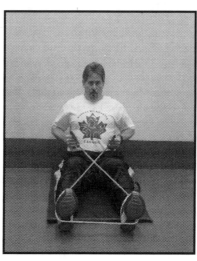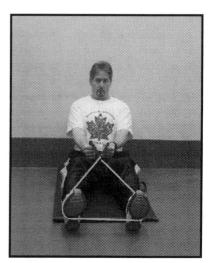

Sit on the floor with your feet hip width apart. Wrap the resistance tubing securely under both feet. Cross the resistance tubing and hold one handle in each hand, with your palms inward towards the ribs. Row back to full range of motion and avoid excessive sway of the hips or upper body. Return to the start position, and repeat.

Resistance Tubing – Bicep Curl

(Biceps)

In the standing position, place the resistance tubing securely under both feet. Hold one handle in each hand, palms facing forward. Ensure that your elbows stay in a fixed position, at your ribs. Pull your palms up to your shoulders. Return to the start position, and repeat.

NOTE: This exercise can also be done with dumbbells, a curl bar or a straight bar with weights.

Resistance Tubing – Tricep Extensions

(Triceps)

Reverse View

In the standing position, hold one handle of the resistance tubing in your right hand, with your elbow pointing to the ceiling. Secure the tension on the resistance tubing with your left hand (see the reverse view). Extend your right hand to the ceiling. Return to the start position, and repeat. Switch sides, and repeat.

Resistance Tubing – Seated Overhead Press

(Upper Trapezius & Mid Deltoids)

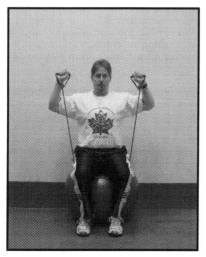

Sit on the stability ball and secure the resistance tubing under your thighs. Hold one handle in each hand, with your palms forward and upper arms parallel to the floor. Press upward, bringing your thumbs together. Return to the start position, and repeat.

Resistance Tubing – Side Laterals

(Side Deltoids)

From a lunge position, secure the resistance tubing under one foot. Hold one handle in each hand, with your palms facing towards the side of your legs. Ensure that there is equal tension on each side. Raise your arms to the side of your body to shoulder height. Return to the start position, and repeat.

Resistance Tubing – Front Delt Raise

(Front Deltoids)

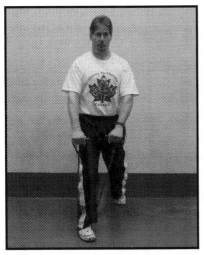

From a lunge position, secure the resistance tubing under one foot. Hold one handle in each hand, with your palms facing towards the front of your thighs. Ensure that there is equal tension on each side. Raise your arms in front of your body to shoulder height. Return to the start position, and repeat.

Resistance Tubing – Reverse Flyes

(Rear Deltoids)

Position your body by placing the resistance tubing securely under both feet, hip width apart. Your upper body is in the bent over position, parallel to the floor. Hold one handle in each hand, palms facing towards the sides of your legs. Ensure that there is equal tension on each side. Raise your arms until they are parallel to the floor. Return to the start position, and repeat.

Pilates – Shoulder Exercise *(Done very slowly)*

(Entire Shoulder Rotator Cuff Region – *Optional Shoulder Work*)

1. Start Position.

2. Press cut rotating palms downward.

3. Raise to ceiling thumbs together.

4. Begin arc downward.

5. Stop level to floor.

6. Squeeze together in flye motion.

7. Return to start position, and repeat.

Pilates – Shoulder & Bicep Exercise *(Done very slowly)*

(Shoulder & Bicep Region - *Optional*)

1. Start position.

2. Bring arms inward pinky fingers together.

3. Extend downward until parallel to floor.

4. Bicep curl upward.

5. Return to start position, and repeat.

Resistance Tubing – Jab/Cross Speed Round

(Warm-Up - *Optional*)

With the resistance tubing going around your back and under your arms, assume the boxer stance. Hold one handle in each hand and ensure that there is sufficient tension on the resistance tubing to work the muscles and avoid hyperextension. Perform jab/cross techniques with speed and proper technique. Switch legs, and repeat.

NOTE: This warm-up can be performed for 15-20 seconds on each side, and repeated as many times as you wish. This exercise builds strength and endurance in punching.

Resistance Tubing – Uppercut Speed Round

(Warm-Up - *Optional*)

With the resistance tubing securely under one foot, assume the boxer stance. Hold one handle in each hand and ensure that there is sufficient tension on the resistance tubing to work the muscles. Perform uppercut techniques with speed and proper technique. Switch legs, and repeat.

NOTE: This warm-up can be performed for 15-20 seconds on each side, and repeated as many times as you wish. This exercise builds strength and endurance in punching.

Toe Tappers

(Upper & Lower Abs)

Lie flat on your back with your knees bent, and your shoulders and toes on the floor. Simultaneously rise up, bringing your knees and elbows together. Lower back down to the start position, allowing your shoulders and toes to only tap the floor, keeping constant contraction on your abdominal muscles. Repeat.

NOTE: This exercise can be done with or without a medicine ball.

Side-to-Side

(Obliques)

1. Sit balanced on buttocks with medicine ball held chest high.

2. Touch the medicine ball to the floor on the right.

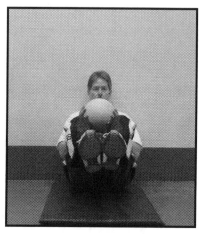

3. Return to start position.

4. Touch the medicine ball to the floor on the left.

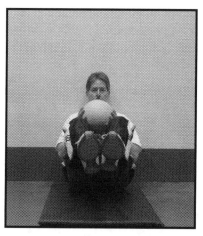

5. Return to start position, and repeat.

NOTES : This exercise can be done with or without a medicine ball.

To decrease the level of difficulty, you can have your heels touching the floor.

Jack Knifes

(Lower Abominals)

Lie flat on your back with your legs raised 90 degrees from the floor, and your arms outstretched above your head. Maintaining your leg position, reach up as high as you can towards your feet. Lower back down to the start position, and repeat.

NOTE: This exercise can be done with or without a medicine ball.

Roll-Ups

(Upper Abdominals)

Lie flat on your back with your knees bent, and your shoulders and toes on the floor. Place the medicine ball on your abdominals. Slowly roll the medicine ball up your thighs, bringing your shoulders off the floor, contracting the upper abdominal muscles. Lower back down to the start position, and repeat.

V-Sit Bicycles

(Upper & Lower Abdominals)

Sit balanced on your buttocks with one leg bent, and the other leg straight out. With your hands in the guard position, alternate touching your elbow to the opposite knee, while maintaining your balance and keeping both feet off the floor.

NOTE: To decrease the level of difficulty, this exercise can be done in the lying position.

Heal to Toe Punches

(Upper Abdominals)

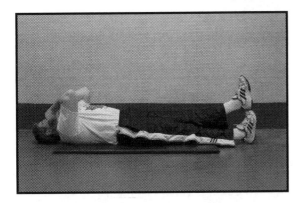

Lie flat on your back with your legs outstretched, and your hands in the guard position. Place your left heel on your right toe. Raise your shoulders 4-6 inches off the floor, contracting your upper abdominal muscles. From this locked position, throw a left jab and then a right cross. Go back to the guard position, lower your shoulders back to the start position, and repeat. Switch feet, and repeat.

Up & Out

(Lower Abdominals & Groin)

1. Lie flat on your back with your legs bent in a 90 degree position.

2. Push your feet to the ceiling.

3. Return back to start position.

4. Push your legs straight out, keeping them 2-6 inches off the floor.

5. Return to the start position, and repeat

One Legged Plank

(Entire Core & Back)

Lie face down on the floor, placing your forearms on the floor and lock your body level to the floor in a plank position. Place your left toe on your right heel and hold the position. Switch sides, and repeat. Start by holding this position for 10 seconds, and work your way up to 60 seconds.

NOTE: To decrease the level of difficulty, this exercise can be done with both feet on the floor, with legs together or apart.

One Armed Plank

(Core & Obliques)

Lie face down on the floor, supporting yourself on one arm. Ensure that your shoulders are parallel to the floor and hold the position. Switch sides, and repeat. Start by holding this position for 10 seconds, and work your way up to 60 seconds.

Side Oblique Plank

(Obliques)

Lie on your side on the floor, supporting yourself on your forearm. Keep your legs straight, one on top of the other, and hold by contracting the obliques. Switch sides, and repeat. Start by holding this position for 10 seconds, and work your way up to 60 seconds.

One Legged Plank with Knee Strike – Rear Kick

(Core & Legs)

Lie face down on the floor, supporting yourself on both arms. Ensure that your shoulders are parallel to the floor. Slowly perform a knee strike movement and then extend the leg backward and upward in a rear kick movement. Repeat. Switch sides, and repeat.

Oblique Plank with Elbow Touch

(Obliques)

Lie on your side on the floor, supporting yourself on your forearm, in the oblique plank position. Keep your legs straight, one on top of the other. Bring your hand to your ear, with your elbow pointing towards the ceiling. Bring your elbow to the floor in front of your body. Return to the full plank position, and repeat. Switch sides, and repeat.

CHAPTER EIGHTEEN

Stretching Exercises

....

Stretching

Each stretch should be held in position for 10-30 seconds. You should feel mild discomfort. Do not bounce. Breath comfortably, exhaling as you elongate the muscle group.

Glutes & Groin :
    Toes pointed out 45 degrees,
    heels under hips.

Hamstrings :
    Shift, positioning heel to floor,
    toes up.

Glutes :
    Full squat ensuring thighs are
    parallel to floor, toes forward, feet
    slightly wider than hip width apart.

Adductors :
    Toes forward, shift body to side,
    feel stretch on inside of extended leg.

Hamstring & Calf :
Leg extended, heel to floor, toe up. Supporting leg slightly bent.

Shin-Anterior Tibialis :
Press toe towards floor, stretching the shin.

Groin, Quads & Glutes :
Bend lead leg forward, bringing torso to thigh, fully extending back leg.

Back & Shoulders :
Interlock fingers, palms forward. Gently push forward, bending at the waist.

Rear Deltoid :
Raise arm parallel to floor. Hand palm down on opposite shoulder. With the other arm gently press to rear.

Rear Deltoid :
Switch sides.

Start Position :
Feet a comfortable
width apart. Extend arms
overhead, palms together.

Obliques :
Slide hand down the side of
the leg, while bringing the
opposite arm up over head.
Do not lean forward or backward.

Palms Together :

Obliques :
Switch sides.

Palms Together :

Top Deltoids & Trapezius :
Press fingers towards floor.

The following twelve moves (on this and the facing page) are done as one series of stretches.

Start Position :
Feet a comfortable width apart. Palms together.

Pectorals :
Press elbows back, palms forward. Upper arms parallel to the floor.

Palms Together :

Front Deltoids & Pecs :
Extend arms out, parallel to floor, palms down. Press fingers to rear.

Palms Together :

Biceps & Pecs :
Extend arms out, parallel to floor, palms forward. Press fingers downward.

(Continued from previous page)

Palms Together :   **Forearms, Biceps & Pecs** : **Palms Together** :
Extend arms out, parallel
to floor, palms up. Press
fingers to rear.

Lats, Trapezuis & **Triceps** :   **Triceps** :
Rhomboids :   Position arm with elbow   Switch sides.
Extend arms over head,   to ceiling. Gently pull the
palms together. Press   arm back behind head.
towards ceiling.

Start Position :
   Fists together, arms
   parallel to the floor.

Obliques & Rear Deltoids:
   Rotate torso to the right.

Fists Together :
   Bring torso back to centre.

Obliques & Rear Deltoids :
   Rotate torso to the left.

Fists Together :
   Bring torso back to centre.

CHAPTER NINETEEN

Sample Workout

Warm-Up

- Head side to side
- Shoulders forward and back circular
- Shuffle forward and back
- Add a Jab
- Jab Cross
- Pivots
- Pivot Jab

- Pivot Jab Cross
- Add Hook and Uppercut
- Switch sides and repeat
- Jack and Jab X 4
- Jack and Jab X 2
- Jack and Jab X 1
- Rear Knee Strikes 20 each side

Stretching (After Warm-Up)

- Hamstring & Calves
- Lunge stretch (Front)
- Side Lunge into heel to floor toe raise
- Straddle stance Sumo stretch

- Straddle splits
- Standing lateral trunk stretch
- Tricep stretch
- Bicep stretch

NOTE: Two 3-minute rounds of skipping can be utilized as the warm-up segment.

Resistance Training

- Squats
- Lunges
- Side Step Adductor
- Ball Squeeze
- Bench Press
- Flyes
- Seated Two Arm Row

- Overhead Press
- Bicep Curls
- Tricep Extensions
- Toe Tappers
- Side-to-Side
- Jack Knifes
- Planks Feet together & Feet Apart

Optional Cardio Combinations

(Air Attack Only - Without Partner Pad Holding)

Boxing Combinations

Jab, Cross
Jab, Jab, Cross
Jab, Jab, Cross
Switch sides repeat

Jab, Cross
Jab, Cross, Hook, Hook
Switch sides repeat
Shuffle-Shuffle-Shuffle-Cross
Add Jabs with hand to side you are advancing

Advancing Jab, Jab, Jab, Cross (Hold)
Repeat back Switch sides repeat
Same add Cross, Jab, Cross (3 jabs back)

Finish with repeat of Jack & Jab & Stretch

Kickboxing Combinations

Jab, Cross
Jab, Jab, Cross
Jab, Jab, Cross, 2 Rear Knees
Switch sides repeat

Jab, Cross, Hook, Hook
Jab, Cross, Rear Knee Strike, Hook
Switch sides repeat
Shuffle-Shuffle-Shuffle-Cross
Add Jabs with hand to side you are advancing

Advancing Jab, Jab, Jab, Cross (Hold)
Repeat back Switch sides repeat
Advancing Right knee-Left knee, 3 jabs back
Switch sides repeat
Same add Cross, Jab, Cross (3 jabs back)

Rear Leg Knee Strikes (Both Legs)
Squat and Kick (Both legs)
Lead Leg Snap kicks (Both legs)
Rear Leg Snap Kicks (Both legs)
Lead Leg Round Kicks (Both Legs)
Rear Leg Round House Kicks (Both Legs)

Finish with repeat of Jack & Jab & Stretch

Pad Drills

Punching Pad Drills

Left Foot Forward	10 Jabs
Right Foot Forward	10 Jabs
Left Foot Forward	10 Crosses
Right Foot Forward	10 Crosses
Left Foot Forward	10 Jab-Cross
Right Foot Forward	10 Jab-Cross
Left Foot Forward	10 Jab-Cross, Hook, Hook
Right Foot Forward	10 Jab-Cross, Hook, Hook
Left Foot Forward	10 Jab, Jab, Duck, Cross
Right Foot Forward	10 Jab, Jab, Duck, Cross
Left Foot Forward	10 Jab, Cross, Hook, Uppercut
Right Foot Forward	10 Jab, Cross, Hook, Uppercut

Kicking Pad Drills

Squat & Kick 20 reps

Left Foot Forward	10 Front Snap Kicks
Right Foot Forward	10 Front Snap Kicks
Left Foot Forward	10 Round Kicks
Right Foot Forward	10 Round Kicks
Left Foot Forward	10 Rear Leg Snap Kicks
Right Foot Forward	10 Rear Leg Snap Kicks
Left Foot Forward	10 Roundhouse Kicks
Right Foot Forward	10 Roundhouse Kicks
Left Foot Forward	10 Rear Leg Knee Strikes
Right Foot Forward	10 Rear Leg Knee Strikes

NOTE: Not all drills need to be performed, mix it up for variety. You need not use reps, utilizing 15 second time increments allows you to go at your own pace accommodating your fitness and skill level.

Beginner Combinations: Switching Foot Positions

Boxing Combinations

Left Foot Forward   Jabs
Right Foot Forward Jabs
Left Foot Forward   Jab, Cross
Right Foot Forward Jab, Cross
Left Foot Forward   Jab, Jab, Cross
Right Foot Forward Jab, Jab, Cross
Left Foot Forward   Jab, Cross, Jab, Cross
Right Foot Forward Jab, Cross, Jab, Cross
Left Foot Forward   Jab, Cross, Hook
Right Foot Forward Jab, Cross, Hook
Left Foot Forward   Jab, Cross, Hook, Hook
Right Foot Forward Jab, Cross, Hook, Hook
Left Foot Forward   Jab, Jab, Duck, Cross
Right Foot Forward Jab, Jab, Duck, Cross
Left Foot Forward   Jab, Jab, Cross, Cross
Right Foot Forward Jab, Jab, Cross, Cross
Left Foot Forward   Jab, Cross, Jab, Cross, Hook
Right Foot Forward Jab, Cross, Jab, Cross, Hook
Left Foot Forward   Jab, Cross, Jab, Cross, Hook, Uppercut
Right Foot Forward Jab, Cross, Jab, Cross, Hook, Uppercut

Kickboxing Combinations

Left Foot Forward   Jab, Rear Knee Strike
Right Foot Forward Jab, Rear Knee Strike
Left Foot Forward   Jab, Cross, Lead Leg Snap Kick
Right Foot Forward Jab, Cross, Lead Leg Snap Kick
Left Foot Forward   Jab, Jab, Cross, Lead Leg Snap Kick
Right Foot Forward Jab, Jab, Cross, Lead Leg Snap Kick
Left Foot Forward   Lead Leg Snap Kick, Jab, Cross
Right Foot Forward Lead Leg Snap Kick, Jab, Cross
Left Foot Forward   Jab, Cross, Hook, Rear Knee Strike
Right Foot Forward Jab, Cross, Hook, Rear Knee Strike
Left Foot Forward   Jab, Cross, Hook, Lead Leg Snap Kick
Right Foot Forward Jab, Cross, Hook, Lead Leg Snap Kick
Left Foot Forward   Lead Leg Round Kick, Cross, Hook
Right Foot Forward Lead Leg Round Kick, Cross, Hook

(Continued on next page)

Kickboxing Combinations (Continued)

Left Foot Forward   Lead Leg Snap Kick, Jab, Jab, Cross, Cross
Right Foot Forward Lead Leg Snap Kick, Jab, Jab, Cross, Cross
Left Foot Forward   Jab, Cross, Hook, Rear Leg Round House Kick
Right Foot Forward Jab, Cross, Hook, Rear Leg Round House Kick
Left Foot Forward   Lead Leg Snap Kick, Lead Leg Round Kick, Jab, Cross
Right Foot Forward Lead Leg Snap Kick, Lead Leg Round Kick, Jab, Cross
Left Foot Forward   Jab, Cross, Jab, Cross, Cross, Hook, Rear Knee Strike
Right Foot Forward Jab, Cross, Jab, Cross, Cross, Hook, Rear Knee Strike

NOTE : After the final round take a two minute active break to walk around and let your heart rate come down, towel off and drink water.

Heavy Bag or Free Standing Bag Training Combinations

Jabs with rear hand in guard position.
Crosses with lead hand in guard position.

Jab, Cross
Jab, Cross, Jab, Cross
Jab, Cross, Hook
Jab, Cross, Hook, Uppercut
Jab, Cross, Hook, Hook
Jab, Uppercut
Jab, Uppercut, Hook
Jab, Uppercut, Hook, Cross
Jab, Jab, Duck, Cross

Front Kicks as the bag swings back to you repeat the kick.
Front Round Kicks as the bag swings back to you repeat the kick.
Rear Leg Front Kicks as the bag swings back to you repeat the kick.
Rear Leg Roundhouse Kicks as the bag swings back repeat the kick.

Jab, Roundhouse
Jab, Cross, Hook, Lead Leg Round Kick
Front Kick, Roundhouse, Jab, Cross
Front Kick, Jab, Cross, Roundhouse
Round Kick, Jab, Cross, Rear Leg Front Kick
Rear Leg Front Kick, Roundhouse Kick
Lead Leg Front Kick, Roundhouse
Rear Leg Roundhouse, Jab, Jab, Cross
Jab, Cross, Jab, Cross, 2 Rear Leg Front Kicks

NOTE : Add flurries of 8-10 punch, kick or punch and kick combinations. Bag work is best done in simulated round segments or 15 second repetitive action with 15 seconds active rest.

Abs, Back & Upper Body Floor-Work Exercises

- Knees up elbows to knees
  (Calves parallel to floor, thighs 90 degrees, raise up elbows to knees)
- Toe taps
  (Lay on back, raise feet and upper body touching elbows to knees)
- Bicycle elbow to knee
  (Lay on back, alternate extending legs in bicycle motion touching elbows to knees)
- Palms up arms extended crunch
  (Calves parallel to floor, thighs 90 degrees, palms up, push fingers forward while raising up)
- Alternate knee to elbow, leg extended on back
  (Same as bicycle only one leg at a time)
- Bridge on back, 2 legs , 1 leg
  (Arms folded across chest, push hips up)
- Table tops, one arm, two arms, one leg raised
  (Body parallel to floor support by one forearm or two forearms)
- Push-ups
  (Traditional form, wide or narrow hand position or knuckles with or without gloves)
- Back extensions
  (Lying face down raise torso and legs simultaneously)
- Left side oblique raises and hold 8
  (Supported on forearm, legs stacked balancing on the side of the feet)
- Right side oblique raises and hold 8
  (Repeat on right side)

Stretching

- Hamstring & calves
- Lunge stretch (front)
- Side lunge into heel to floor toe raise
- Straddle stance stretch
- Straddle splits
- Standing lateral trunk stretch
- Tricep stretch
- Bicep stretch

CHAPTER TWENTY

Beginner Workouts & Journals

First 8–12 Weeks ≈ 2–3 Sessions per week

Warm-Up & Combinations

 2 rounds skipping (Warm-up)
(2 minute rounds, 1 minute rest between rounds)

 1 round shadow boxing and foot work *(p.52-54)*
(2 minute round, 1 minute rest)

 2 rounds punch combinations on heavy bag or
partner pad work *(p.66-68)*
(2 minute rounds, 1 minute rest between rounds)

 1 round kick combinations on heavy bag or
kick shield with partner *(p.60-62)*
(2 minute round, 1 minute rest)

 2 rounds punch & kick combinations on the heavy bag or
partner pad work *(p.69-84)*
(2 minute rounds, 1 minute rest between rounds)

Resistance Training Exercises

 Squats *(p.90)*

 Bicep Curl *(p.96)*

 Lunges *(p.90)*

 Tricep Extensions *(p.97)*

 Bench Press *(p.94)*

 Toe Tappers *(p.103)*

 Seated Two *(p.96)* Arm Row

 Jack Knifes *(p.105)*

 Overhead Press *(p.98)*

 Planks - Feet *(p.109)* Together

NOTE : Full body exercises with 1-2 sets of 12-15 reps of each exercise using resistance band, stability ball, medicine ball and free-body, including core, abs and back exercises.

Photocopy the following pages and keep track of your program.

Goals

Date: _____

SHORT-TERM GOALS :

_____

_____

_____

_____

_____

_____

_____

Reward : _____

LONG-TERM GOALS :

_____

_____

_____

_____

_____

_____

_____

_____

_____

_____

_____

_____

_____

_____

_____

_____

Reward : _____

Daily Journal

Date: _____

SLEEP :

How much sleep did you get last night? _____

NUTRITION :

Describe what and when you ate and drank throughout the day.

Breakfast: _____

Lunch: _____

Dinner: _____

Snacks: _____

_____

Water: _____

_____

Other Physical Activities: _____

_____

_____

RESULTS :

Describe how you felt throughout the day. How did you feel: upon waking up; before and after your workout; mid afternoon, etc? Did you feel: fatigued, invigorated, drowsy, alert, proud of yourself, disappointed, etc?

_____

_____

_____

_____

_____

_____

_____

Workout Chart

Date: _____

WARM-UP	ROUNDS	REST
Skipping	2 rounds - each 2 minutes	1 minute between rounds
Shadow Boxing	1 round - 2 minutes	1 minute after round

COMBINATIONS : In each "Round" column, enter the time of the round (to a maximum of 2 minutes) and describe the type of exercise (heavy bag, focus pads, etc.) For example: *1 1/2 minutes heavy bag*

COMBINATIONS	ROUND ONE	ROUND TWO
Punch Combos		
Kick Combos		
Punch & Kick Combos		

RESISTANCE TRAINING	NUMBER OF REPS	NUMBER OF SETS
Squats		
Lunges		
Bench Press		
Seated Two Row Arm		

RESISTANCE TRAINING *(Cont'd)*	NUMBER OF REPS	NUMBER OF SETS
Overhead Press		
Bicep Curls		
Tricep Extensions		

AB WORKOUT	NUMBER OF REPS	NUMBER OF SETS
Toe Tappers		
Jack Knifes		
Planks - Feet Together		

COOL-DOWN STRETCHES	*Remember to stretch each body part worked*

CHAPTER TWENTY-ONE

Contender Workouts & Journals

....

From 12–20 Weeks ≈ 3–4 Sessions per week

Warm-Up & Combinations

 2 rounds skipping (Warm-up)
(2 minute rounds, 1 minute rest between rounds)

 2 rounds shadow boxing and foot work *(p.52-54)*
(2 minutes round, 1 minute rest between rounds)

 2 rounds punch combinations on heavy bag or
partner pad work *(p.66-68)*
(2 minute rounds, 1 minute rest between rounds)

 2 rounds kick combinations on heavy bag or
kick shield with partner *(p.60-62)*
(2 minute rounds, 1 minute rest between rounds)

 2 rounds punch & kick combinations on the heavy bag or
partner pad work *(p.69-84)*
(2 minute rounds, 1 minute rest between rounds)

Resistance Training Exercises

 Squats *(p.90)*

 Lunges *(p.90)*

 Side Step Adductors *(p.93)*

 Squeeze & Punch *(p.92)*

 Bench Press *(p.94)*

 Flyes *(p.95)*

 Seated Two *(p.96)* Arm Row

 Overhead Press *(p.98)*

 Bicep Curls *(p.96)*

 Tricep Extensions *(p.97)*

 Toe Tappers *(p.103)*

 Side-to-Side *(p.104)*

 Jack Knifes *(p.105)*

 Planks - Feet Apart & *(p.109)* Together

NOTE : Full body exercises with 1-2 sets of 12-15 reps of each exercise using resistance band, stability ball, medicine ball and free-body, including core, abs and back exercises.

Photocopy the following pages and keep track of your program.

Goals

Date: _____

SHORT-TERM GOALS :

_____
_____
_____
_____
_____
_____
_____

Reward : _____

LONG-TERM GOALS :

_____
_____
_____
_____
_____
_____
_____
_____
_____
_____
_____
_____
_____
_____
_____
_____
_____

Reward : _____

Daily Journal

Date: _____

SLEEP :

How much sleep did you get last night? _____

NUTRITION :

Describe what and when you ate and drank throughout the day.

Breakfast: _____

Lunch: _____

Dinner: _____

Snacks: _____

_____

Water: _____

_____

Other Physical Activities: _____

_____

_____

RESULTS :

Describe how you felt throughout the day. How did you feel: upon waking up; before and after your workout; mid afternoon, etc? Did you feel: fatigued, invigorated, drowsy, alert, proud of yourself, disappointed, etc?

_____

_____

_____

_____

_____

_____

_____

Workout Chart

Date: _____

WARM-UP	ROUNDS	REST
Skipping	2 rounds - each 2 minutes	1 minute between rounds
Shadow Boxing	2 rounds - each 2 minutes	1 minute between rounds

COMBINATIONS : In each "Round" column, enter the time of the round (to a maximum of 2 minutes) and describe the type of exercise (heavy bag, focus pads, etc.) For example: *1 1/2 minutes heavy bag*

COMBINATIONS	ROUND ONE	ROUND TWO
Punch Combos		
Kick Combos		
Punch & Kick Combos		

RESISTANCE TRAINING	NUMBER OF REPS	NUMBER OF SETS
Squats		
Lunges		
Side Step Adductor		
Ball Squeeze & Punch		
Bench Press		

RESISTANCE TRAINING *(Cont'd)*	NUMBER OF REPS	NUMBER OF SETS
Flyes		
Seated Two Row Arm		
Overhead Press		
Bicep Curls		
Tricep Extensions		

AB WORKOUT	NUMBER OF REPS	NUMBER OF SETS
Toe Tappers		
Side-to-Side		
Jack Knifes		
Planks - Feet Apart & Together		

COOL-DOWN STRETCHES	*Remember to stretch each body part worked*

CHAPTER TWENTY-TWO

Champ Workouts & Journals

From 12–20 Weeks ≈ 3–4 Sessions per week

Warm-Up & Combinations

 3 rounds skipping (Warm-up)
(3 minute rounds, 1 minute rest between rounds)

 2 rounds shadow boxing and foot work *(p.52-54)*
(3 minutes round, 1 minute rest between rounds)

 2 rounds punch combinations on heavy bag or
partner pad work *(p.66-68)*
(3 minute rounds, 1 minute rest between rounds)

 2 rounds kick combinations on heavy bag or
kick shield with partner *(p.60-62)*
(3 minute rounds, 1 minute rest between rounds)

 3 rounds punch & kick combinations on the heavy bag or
partner pad work *(p.69-84)*
(3 minute rounds, 1 minute rest between rounds)

Resistance Training Exercises

Split your resistance training routine - Upper Body one day - Lower Body the next.
Do the exercises with 2-3 sets of 12-15 reps of each exercise.

DAY ONE	DAY TWO

 Squats *(p.90)*

 Lunges *(p.90)*

 Side Step Adductors *(p.93)*

 Squeeze & Punch *(p.92)*

 Side Kicks *(p.91)*

 Roundhouse Kicks *(p.91)*

 Rear kicks *(p.110)*

 Bench Press *(p.94)*

 Flyes *(p.95)*

 Seated Two Arm Row *(p.96)*

 Seated Lat Row *(p.95)*

 Overhead Press *(p.98)*

 Side Laterals *(p.98)*

 Reverse Flyes *(p.99)*

 Side Laterals *(p.98)*

 Front Arm Raises *(p.99)*

 Bicep Curls *(p.96)*

 Tricep Extensions *(p.97)*

Alternate Split Routine Workouts

Day One

All punch combinations with speed for cardio either air attack, heavy bag or pad work, (number of rounds to be determined by fitness and skill level) combined with 1 set of 15 reps of each lower body exercises using resistance band, stability ball, medicine ball and free-body, including core, abs and back exercises as well as stretching.

Day Two

All kick combinations with speed for cardio either air attack, heavy bag or pad work, (number of rounds to be determined by fitness and skill level) combined with 1 set of 15 reps of each upper body exercises using resistance band, stability ball, medicine ball and free-body, including core, abs and back exercises as well as stretching.

Day Three

All punch and kick combinations with heavy bag and pad work, (number of rounds to be determined by fitness and skill level). Include core, abs and back exercises as well as stretching.

Day Four

Full body exercises with 2-3 sets of 12-15 reps of each exercise using resistance band, stability ball, medicine ball and free-body, including core, abs and back exercises as well as stretching.

Day Five

REST

This program does not have to be performed on sequential days; you can give yourself a day off between workouts. To modify the program utilize the F.I.T.T. principle. As you increase or decrease any of the components, Frequency, Intensity, Time or Type you effectively modify the program to match your fitness level. See "Cardiovascular Efficiency" on page 7.

Do not over-train as you will diminish the progress and make yourself susceptible to injuries.

Photocopy the following pages and keep track of your program.

Goals

Date: _____

SHORT-TERM GOALS :

_____

_____

_____

_____

_____

_____

_____

Reward : _____

LONG-TERM GOALS :

_____

_____

_____

_____

_____

_____

_____

_____

_____

_____

_____

_____

_____

_____

_____

_____

_____

Reward : _____

Daily Journal

Date: _____

SLEEP :

How much sleep did you get last night? _____

NUTRITION :

Describe what and when you ate and drank throughout the day.

Breakfast: _____

Lunch: _____

Dinner: _____

Snacks: _____

_____

Water: _____

_____

Other Physical Activities: _____

_____

_____

RESULTS :

Describe how you felt throughout the day. How did you feel: upon waking up; before and after your workout; mid afternoon, etc? Did you feel: fatigued, invigorated, drowsy, alert, proud of yourself, disappointed, etc?

_____

_____

_____

_____

_____

_____

_____

Workout Chart

Date: _____

WARM-UP	ROUNDS	REST
Skipping	3 rounds - each 3 minutes	1 minute between rounds
Shadow Boxing	2 rounds - each 3 minutes	1 minute between rounds

COMBINATIONS : In each "Round" column, enter the time of the round (to a maximum of 3 minutes) and describe the type of exercise (heavy bag, focus pads, etc.) For example: *2 minutes heavy bag*

COMBINATIONS	ROUND ONE	ROUND TWO	ROUND THREE
Punch Combos			
Kick Combos			
Punch & Kick Combos			

REMAINDER OF WORKOUT: Depending on which "Day" you're on, enter the type of exercise you're doing in the first column of the following charts. For example: *on Day Two your first two Resistance Training exercises would be "Bench Press" and "Flyes"*.

RESISTANCE TRAINING	NUMBER OF REPS	NUMBER OF SETS

RESISTANCE TRAINING *(Cont'd)*	NUMBER OF REPS	NUMBER OF SETS

AB WORKOUT	NUMBER OF REPS	NUMBER OF SETS

COOL-DOWN STRETCHES	*Remember to stretch each body part worked*

The Ultimate
Fitness Boxing & Kickboxing
Workout

Printed in the United States
By Bookmasters